ANCIENT GREECE AND ROME:
MYTHS AND BELIEFS

WORLD MYTHOLOGIES

ANCIENT GREECE AND ROME: MYTHS AND BELIEFS

Tony Allan and Sara Maitland

ROSEN
PUBLISHING®

New York

This edition published in 2012 by:

The Rosen Publishing Group, Inc.
29 East 21st Street
New York, NY 10010

Library of Congress Cataloging-in Publication Data

Allan, Tony, 1946–
Ancient Greece and Rome: myths and beliefs/Tony Allan, Sara Maitland.
    p. cm.—(World mythologies)
Includes bibliographical references (p.   ) and index.
ISBN 978-1-4488-5993-1 (library binding)
1. Mythology, Classical. 2. Greece—Religion. 3. Rome—Religion. I. Maitland, Sara, 1950– II. Title.
BL723.A45 2012
292—dc23

                                2011037146

Manufactured in the United States of America

CPSIA Compliance Information: Batch #W12YA: For further information, contact Rosen Publishing, New York, New York, at 1-800-237-9932.

© 1997 Duncan Baird Publishers

Photo Credits:

The publisher would like to thank the following people, museums and photographic libraries for permission to reproduce their material. Every care has been taken to trace copyright holders. However, if we have omitted anyone we apologize and will, if informed, make corrections in any future edition.

Key: a above; **b** below; **c** centrer; **l** left; **r** right

Abbreviations:

AAA: Ancient Art and Architecture Collection, London
AKG: Archiv für Kunst und Geschichte, London
BAL: Bridgeman Art Library, London
BM: British Museum, London

ETA: e.t. archive, London
MH: Michael Holford, London
RHPL: Robert Harding Picture Library, London
WFA: Werner Forman Archive, London

6 BM; **7** ETA/Archaeological Museum of Naples; **8** MH/BM; **11** MH/BM; **12** WFA; **13** WFA/BM; **15** AKG/Erich Lessing; **16** Sonia Halliday Photographs/Bardo Museum, Tunis; **18l** BM;**18r** AKG/Staatliche Antikensammlung, Munich; **18b** BM;**19t** Sonia Halliday Photographs;**19c** AKG/Erich Lessing; **19b** MH/Marquis of Northampton; **20** AKG/Erich Lessing; **21** AKG/Badisches Landesmuseum, Karlsruhe; **22** AAA; **24** BM; **25** CMD; **26** ETA; **27l** CMD; **27r** Sonia Halliday Photographs; **28** MH/BM; **29** AKG/Erich Lessing; **30** The Travel Library; **31** R.J.A.Wilson/Berlin Museum; **32** AKG/Erich Lessing; **33** BAL/Palazzo dei Normani, Palermo; **34** WFA; **35** MH/BM; **36** CMD; **37** BAL/Vatican Museums and Art Galleries; **39** BAL/Musée des Beaux Arts, Angers; **40** CMD; **41** WFA/BM; **42** CMD; **43** AKG/Erich Lessing; **44** CMD; **45** RHPL; **46** AKG/John Hiss; **47** ETA/Archaeological Museum, Naples; **48** AAA/Ronald Sheridan; **49** AKG/Erich Lessing; **50** CMD; **51** Zefa; **52** CMD; **53** R.J.A.Wilson/Antikenmuseum, Basle; **54** AAA/Ronald Sheridan; **55** AAA/Ronald Sheridan; **56** AKG/Erich Lessing; **58** ETA/Archaeological Museum, Verona; **59** CMD; **60l** ETA/Uffizi, Florence; **60r** BAL/Giraudon/Musée des Beaux Arts, Nantes; **61al** BAL/National Gallery, London; **61r** BAL/Uffizi, Florence; **61b** BAL/Villa Farnesina, Rome; **62** AKG/Erich Lessing; **63** AAA/Ronald Sheridan; **64** AAA/Ronald Sheridan; **65** AAA/Ronald Sheridan; **66** WFA/Archaeological Museum, Naples; **67** AAA/Ronald Sheridan; **68** ETA/National Museum, Athens; **69** BM; **70** MH/BM; **72** CMD; **73** ETA; **74** Zefa; **75t** Zefa; **75b** MH/BM; **76** ETA/Ephesus Museum,Turkey; **77** ETA/Archaeological Museum, Naples; **79** AAA/Ronald Sheridan; **81** MH/BM; **82** WFA/Antiquario Palatino, Rome; **83** Zefa; **84** ETA/Villa Giulia, Rome; **85** AAA/Ronald Sheridan; **86** CMD; **88** CMD; **89** Scala/Museo Nazionale delle Terme, Rome; **90** Scala/Museo Gregoriano, Rome; **91** WFA; **92** ETA/Museo Nazionale delle Terme, Rome; **93** ETA/Historical Museum, Sofia; **94** MH/BM; **95** AKG/Erich Lessing; **98** Scala/Museo Eoliano, Lipari; **99** R.J.A.Wilson; **100** AAA/Ronald Sheridan; **101** Hirmer Fotoarchiv/Antikensammlungen, Munich; **102** Scala/Archaeological Museum de Pegli, Genoa; **103** AKG/Erich Lessing; **104** BM; **105** ETA; **106** BM; **108** ETA/Museo Etrusco, Volterra; **109** AAA/Ronald Sheridan; **110** BM; **111** BAL/BM; **112-113** Zefa; **114tl** ET/Archaeological Museum, Naples; **114tr** and **b** Zefa; **115** ETA; **116** BAL/National Gallery London; **117** AAA/Ronald Sheridan; **118** BM; **119** Sonia Halliday Photographs; **121** BAL/Louvre, Paris; **122** BAL/Lauros-Giraudon; **123** The Mansell Collection; **124** ETA; **126** AKG/Erich Lessing; **127** MH/BM; **128** Scala/Museo Gregoriano Etrusco, Rome; **129** BM; **130** ETA; **131** Sonia Halliday Photographs; **134** Images Colour Library; **135** ETA/Victoria and Albert Museum, London; **136** RHPL/Michael J. Howell; **137** Popperfoto

Contents

A Maenad with snakes in her hair, decorating a Greek bowl *c.* 490 BCE.

THE CLASSICAL WORLD

The presence of the Olympian gods around us still—in art and literature, in language, in scientific and psychological terminology, and in the names we have for the heavenly bodies—is a tribute to the power of the classical, and particularly the Greek, creative imagination. Stories originally conceived more than three millennia ago—of Zeus and Hera, Orpheus and Eurydice, of Pandora's Box—still appeal to, and have meaning for, people throughout the world today.

From the very beginning, the myths showed an extraordinary ability to travel, sometimes great distances. While some were native to Greek soil, others were brought there by invaders from the north. At the same time, the harsh geography of mainland Greece, with its shortage of fertile land, forced emigrants to head outward across the sea. Greek colonies sprang up in regions as distant from each other as southern Italy, Egypt, and the Crimea. And wherever Greek settlers sailed, the tales always journeyed with them.

It was through the Greek colonies in Italy that Romans first encountered the stories, probably in the eighth century BCE. At the time, Rome was simply a small town on the Italian mainland, while Greek civilization was far more advanced. The Italian peoples had few myths of their own, and their gods lacked the elaborate characterizations that distinguished those of the Greeks. Over the centuries, they were content to adopt the stories and beliefs of the newcomers. In many cases, they added little, merely superimposing the names of their own native gods on tales first told of the Olympians on Aegean shores.

Imperial Rome, with its grandiose ambitions, carried the legends of the gods' exploits to regions where even the Greeks had never ventured; at the same time the empire was exposed to fresh foreign influences. However, its dominion eventually crumbled, and new faiths sprang up to take the place of the old religion. Yet somehow the stories themselves survived, outlasting both the gods that were their subject and the people who had once believed in them. They did so because they never lost their relevance over the millennia: like all great myths, they recount universal truths in a memorable fashion, embodying in episodes of love and war the grandest themes of imagination.

Above: **In both Greece and Rome, the gods were commonly honored by animal sacrifice. This fresco from Pompeii, in southern Italy, dating from the 1st century CE, shows a bull being led to the altar.**

Opposite: **This intricate 4th-century Roman silver plate depicts many of the characters of classical mythology.**

7

The Gods of the Greeks

Every four years for more than a millennium, the finest athletes in the Greek-speaking world used to gather at Olympia in the Peloponnese to vie for glory. Founded according to tradition in 776 BCE, the original Olympic Games grew into a five-day celebration of physical achievement in honor of the gods. At their height in the fifth century BCE, up to 40,000 spectators crowded the stadium to cheer on their favorites.

In pageantry and competitiveness there are close parallels between the ancient and modern Olympics, but in one respect the original version was crucially unlike its present-day counterpart. The gathering at Olympia was, in its origins and in much of its ceremonial, a religious festival designed to bring worshippers together to pay homage to the gods. In all, half of the Games' five days were given over to ceremonial and ritual. The religious roots went deep. The site at which the Games were staged was centered on a grove once sacred to the venerable Earth goddess Gaia that at some unknown period had become a cult center for Zeus, chief of the Olympian deities.

In the course of time a great temple to Zeus was built and became the ceremonial centerpiece of the Games. It was then the largest in the Hellenic world. The other focal point for religious ritual at Olympia was a huge altar constructed from the ashes of the cattle sacrificed to Zeus over the years. The meat of the slaughtered beasts was reserved for the thousands of visitors to the Games, who could thus feast and enjoy themselves at the same time as paying respect to the gods.

The quadrennial Olympic celebration of Zeus was one of many thousands of festivals, some big, some small, that were held across the Greek world to honor the gods. The gatherings took many forms. A handful featured athletic contests; others involved activities ranging from dancing and theater to ritual taunting and the punishment of offenders. But the great majority simply consisted of processions, prayers, and sacrifices.

By the time the Olympic Games had taken root, poets had organized and rationalized the

Stadia were constructed at several sites in Greece to house athletic contests honoring the gods. This one was built in the 5th century BCE at Delphi, the oracular shrine, for the Pythian Games in honor of Apollo.

TIME LINE OF THE CLASSICAL WORLD

Ancient Greece

| MINOAN PERIOD 3000—1100 BCE | **3000** |

2000

Destruction of Knossos **1400**

| MYCENAEAN PERIOD 1600—1100 BCE |

Destruction of Troy **1250**

| DARK AND GEOMETRIC AGES 1100–730 BCE | **1000** |

The first Olympic Games **776**
Homer **c. 750**

Olympic wreath

| ARCHAIC PERIOD 730—500 BCE |

First stone temple at Sparta **725**
Hesiod active **c. 700**

Thales of Miletus **c. 600**
First Pythian Games at Delphi **586/5**
Institution of the State Dionysia in Athens **545**
The poet Pindar active **c. 500**

| CLASSICAL PERIOD 500—300 BCE |

First play by Aeschylus **c. 498**
First play by Sophocles **468**
Leadership of Pericles in Athens **461–429**
Sculptor Phidias at work **460–420**
Temple of Zeus at Olympia **456**
First play by Euripides **455**
Temple of Poseidon at Paestum **c. 450**
Start of work on the Parthenon **447**
Peloponnesian War **431–404**
Trial of Socrates **399**
Plato's Academy founded **387**
Sculptor Praxiteles at work **370–330**
Rule of Alexander the Great **336–23**

Comedy mask

| HELLENISTIC PERIOD 300—200 BCE |

Foundation of the Museum and Library of Alexandria **295**
Greece becomes part of the Roman Empire **146**

Ancient Rome

| EARLY PERIOD FROM 760 BCE |

753 Legendary founding of Rome by Romulus and Remus

The Roman she-wolf

| ETRUSCAN PERIOD 625–500 BCE |

509 Temple of Jupiter dedicated in Rome

| ROMAN REPUBLIC 500–27 BCE |

498 Temple of Saturn constructed in Rome

Temple of Saturn

Julius Caesar

240 Earliest Latin tragedy
204 Cult of Cybele reaches Rome

58–49 Caesar's Gallic war

| ROMAN EMPIRE 27 BCE—476 CE |

27 Augustus becomes emperor
28–19 Virgil composes the Aeneid
8 BCE Ovid banished; *Metamorphoses* burned
79 CE Eruption of Mt. Vesuvius
122 Construction of Hadrian's Wall in Britain
c. 150 *The Golden Ass* by Apuleius
284 Reorganization of the empire by Diocletian
313 Edict of Milan enforces tolerance of Christians
360–63 Julian the Apostate; brief revival of Pagan religions
393–95 Paganism banned by Theodosius the Great

When Greece was in its heyday, Rome was only one small town among many in Italy. It was exposed to Hellenic influence as Greece established colonies in Italy from the eighth century BCE onward. The rise of Rome coincided with Greece's decline, and eventually the Hellenistic state was incorporated into the new empire ruled from Rome.

0

gods into a divine First Family. This schematization, however, hid great diversity, since in their origins the deities were as various and dispersed as the Greek people themselves.

Some were native to the land: perhaps half of the twelve Olympians had Greek origins. There were also other local gods whose worship continued into classical times. These *chthonioi* dwelled in the bowels of the Earth—their name means "earth spirits"—and were apparently linked both to the fertility of the land and to a cult of the dead.

Other gods, and other stories, were imported over the course of time by waves of immigrants who swarmed into Greece from the north. Scholars argue over how and when the incomers arrived, whether as peaceful settlers infiltrating over a period of decades, or as invading warriors. Archaeologicial evidence suggests two major

periods of disruption, in the latter parts of the third and second millennia BCE respectively. Each left its mark in the shape of settlements razed to the ground. In the wake of the carnage, new settlers made their appearance. Those who came around 2000 BCE apparently introduced the horse to Greece. They soon integrated with the existing population to produce the great Bronze Age Mycenaean civilization recorded in Homer's epics. From its capital, Mycenae in the Peloponnese, it dominated not only mainland Greece but also the Aegean islands apart from Crete.

That society in turn was swept away in a chaotic period around 1200–1100 BCE, when the Hittite kingdom of present-day Turkey and the Minoan civilization on Crete also collapsed. In the collective folk-memory, Mycenae's downfall was associated with the invasions of the Dorians—

Ancient Greece

Important Greek settlements were found not only on mainland Greece and the islands but also all along the coast of the Aegean. Under Alexander the Great, the Hellenistic empire would spread as far as India.

Greek-speakers from beyond the country's northern border whose dialect remained distinct even six centuries later. Thus the Greece of the classical era evolved from the mingling of indigenous peoples and incomers.

The civilization that developed was shaped as much by geography as by history, because the physical layout of the country indelibly affected its political form. Much of the mainland was taken up by mountains, which cut off one valley society from another, favoring the growth of city-states—small, independent communities living off the produce of the surrounding land. The other crucial influence was the sea and its many islands, which made up about one-fifth of Greece's land area. Even the mainland states looked across the water for much of their trade.

There was intense rivalry and frequent warfare among the city-states, yet they also recognized a common Greekness. The principal elements of this cross-border sense of national identity were the Greek language and the worship of the Olympian pantheon.

No one has ever satisfactorily explained just what special ingredient entered the equation to turn this divided world of mini-states into one of the world's most creative civilizations, which planted seeds of intellectual and political progress that are still flowering. All that can be said for certain is that something extraordinary happened in Greece in the sixth and fifth centuries BCE. Greek thinkers, many of them living in settlements on what is now Turkey's western coast, laid the foundations of Western science and metaphysics, while others pioneered historical writing. At the same time generations of poets not only produced magnificent verse but also developed the art of the theater. The dramatists Sophocles, Aeschylus, Euripides, and Aristophanes gave the world tragic and comic plays revived to this day.

The Greeks went into battle well equipped with weapons and armor. This 5th-century BCE bronze helmet was designed to protect against slashing sword strokes.

The place where this cultural ferment made itself felt most keenly was the great city-state of Athens. Nowhere was freedom of thought more eagerly trumpeted, fostered by its fifth-century BCE leader Pericles: creative energy seemed to hum in the very air. Yet progressive Athens was also devout Athens. As well as being home to a greater number of poets and thinkers, the city also had more religious festivals than almost anywhere else: more than one hundred a year, or roughly one every three days. One of them was the Great Dionysia festival that featured four days of plays, at which many now classic works received their first productions.

11

The Greeks felt no contradiction between piety and intellectual liberty, for one of the unusual features of Greek religion was its lack of dogmatism and its tolerance of freedom of thought. Its theology did not derive from a single source, because it had no sacred books or absolute religious authority. Nor was there a rigorous definition of modes of worship or orthodoxy of belief. So, from an early time, philosophers could seek out secular explanations for natural phenomena without fearing reprisal on religious grounds. And if people were persecuted for impiety, it was usually for neglecting ceremonial or ritual duties, not for their opinions about either the rites they performed or the gods they honored.

Wherever the Greeks settled, they constructed temples to their gods. This shrine at Cape Sounion, Greece, dating from *c.* 430 BCE, was dedicated to the sea god Poseidon.

The annual round of festivities and processions central to religious practice had limitations as a vehicle for personal devotion. Sects that allowed for a more personal commitment also existed. The worship of the god Dionysus, imported into Greece from Asia Minor, was one of these; its devotees venerated the deity with wild dancing in the open air. Other influential cults were associated with the Orphic beliefs, derived from works about the origin of the world supposedly composed by the mythical poet and musician Orpheus (see page 109) or his disciples. These writings propounded the doctrine of the transmigration of the soul after death through reincarnation. The activities surrounding another celebrated cult, centered upon Eleusis, a dozen miles from Athens, were similarly esoteric (see page 58).

Such was the religion of ancient Greece in the classical period of the independent city-states: a mixture of stories of gods that can be traced back to the earliest times, ceremonial activities undertaken by citizens as a civic duty, and secretive sects that provided mystical experiences. But the mix reflected the society that molded it, and as the Hellenic world itself evolved, so ideas about the gods changed too.

The decisive event was the meteoric rise of the Macedonian Alexander the Great, who in a career of conquest spanning just twelve years extended Greek civilization far from its Aegean homeland to the very borders of India. For a brief period up to his death in 323 BCE, he created a Greek empire, which even after it broke up amid the squabbling of his successors left an enduring legacy of Greek-speaking settlers and of monuments to Greek culture that stretched from Afghanistan to Spain. Equally significantly, the Alexandrian empire opened up Greece itself to a range of foreign influences that would permanently change the character of its culture—from Hellenic to Hellenistic, in the language of historians. This multicultural Greek domain was different from the original world of the city-states, each wrapped up in its own political concerns.

Sources of Classical Myth

The classical myths grew out of the same fears, doubts, and insecurities that have helped to shape religions around the world. But the form the tales took in Greece, and even the personalities of the gods themselves, bore the hallmark of the poets who first told them.

The question of the origins of the Greek myths has puzzled modern scholars more than it did the ancient Greeks, who had firm ideas on the subject. According to the fifth-century BCE historian Herodotus, the fathers of Greek mythology were the poets Homer and Hesiod. The latter created the first systematic pantheon, in the *Theogony*, or "Origin of the Gods," which influenced all the later classical writers.

The role of ancient Greece's two great Homeric epics, the *Iliad* and the *Odyssey*, was even more fundamental. The picture they painted of a brood of squabbling deities interfering in human affairs to aid their favorites helped fix the image of the gods indelibly in the minds of future writers. Despite their attribution to Homer, the two works in fact derived from a long tradition of oral story-telling that stretched back to the earliest days when traveling bards roamed the land entertaining noble families with tales of war and adventure. Many scholars now question whether Homer himself ever really existed. Others are convinced that an individual poet did shape the *Iliad* and

This stone relief dating from Hellenistic times shows allegorical figures honoring Homer, the man credited with the composition of Greece's two great epic poems.

Odyssey, but concede that much of the material in them was not original; the origins of Greek myth thus stretch back into the time before the tales were written down.

Besides the work of Homer and Hesiod, stories of the gods were collected in the so-called Homeric hymns—anonymous poems once attributed to Homer, but in fact written by various hands between 800 and 400 BCE. Other poets, including Pindar and Bacchylides, chose the gods as subjects, as did the Athenian dramatists, who wove stories of their deeds into commentaries on the moral character of Greek society.

Later generations of classical writers sought to systematize what had gone before. In Alexandria, the Egyptian city founded by and named after the great Greek conqueror, scholars smoothed out inconsistencies in the legends and further schematized relations among the Olympians. Increasingly, the gods ceased to be objects of worship and became subjects for study.

Under the Romans, poets like Ovid mined the myths for material from which to create delightful but wholly secular stories. Ironically, these versions became more popular in later times than the originals; the shift from religion to legend helped to make them more acceptable to Christian readers, and kept the memory of the gods alive long after the cults that had once been based upon them had passed away.

13

The Rise of Rome

While Hellenism was spreading in the east, a new power was making its presence felt in the western Mediterranean world. Rome began as a small town, equivalent in power and influence to one of the less important Greek city-states. It owed its culture largely to a period of rule by the Etruscans, an artistic trading people who occupied the region immediately to its north. In about 500 BCE, the Romans threw out their foreign rulers, establishing instead a republic that was to last four centuries.

By the early third century BCE the Romans were masters of all Italy. The defeat of Carthage, the northern African civilization that was their main military rival, soon after gave them control of the western Mediterranean. By 215 BCE, not much more than a hundred years after the death of Alexander the Great, they were bidding for supremacy in the eastern Mediterranean too. By 146 BCE the whole Greek nation had become a Roman province. At that point the Greek gods might well have paled into insignificance. That they did not do so was largely because the Roman conquerors respected Greek culture as much as they disdained the Greeks' military prowess. Their own gods were for the most part shadowy beings, and few stories were associated with them. As a result, the Romans were happy to link these nebulous figures with the more colorful Greek deities, whose characters were more clearly delineated and whose mythology was more developed.

The Roman Empire

At its height, in the 2nd century CE, the Roman Empire extended as far north as Britain and as far south as the Nile. As they established their far-flung colonies, the Romans spread their own religion and also encountered foreign deities, sometimes absorbing their attendant religious practices.

Rome
Ostia • Alba Longa
Cumae • Pompeii
Carthage •
Troy
• Constantinople
▲ Mt. Ida
Delphi
Athens
• Tyre
• Alexandria

The Roman Empire,
2nd century CE

The Cult of Isis

Greek and Roman religion was open-ended, accepting influences from all over the ancient world. One honored guest was the Egyptian goddess Isis, whose cult spread across the Mediterranean.

This Roman sculpture of Isis, found in Ephesus in Asia Minor, was carved *c.* 170 CE.

Ancient legend told how Isis scoured Egypt to collect the pieces of her brother Osiris's body after he had been dismembered by their evil brother Seth. Magically restored and revived, Osiris descended into the Underworld to rule the kingdom of the dead. The Greeks knew of the legend as early as the fifth century BCE. They saw parallels between the story and that of their nature goddess Demeter, who could not rest until her daughter Persephone was rescued from the Underworld (see pages 56–59), after she was kidnapped by Hades, its god, who wanted her for a wife.

Greek settlers in Egypt soon adopted the goddess's cult. By the second century BCE, texts known as "Praises of Isis" were circulating in the Hellenistic world, lauding the deity as a grieving wife and mother and a friend of those in need.

In time the cult spread to Rome, too, where at the peak of its success in the second century CE it was more popular than any other foreign-inspired mystery religion. Yet sceptics continued to associate it with magic and superstition. In the original version of the story of the Sorcerer's Apprentice, as described in the writings of the satirist Lucian, it is a disciple of Isis who magically commands several brooms and other implements to clean his home— with disastrous results when an untrained assistant later tries to repeat the trick.

The Olympians acquired Roman counterparts. Zeus became Jupiter; Hera, Juno; Aphrodite, Venus; Dionysus, Bacchus; and Hermes, Mercury, the messenger of the gods. Apollo was accepted under his own name, for no Roman divinity resembled him. (Roman equivalents for all relevant Greek mythological figures named in this book are listed on page 138.)

In the course of these identifications, some of the native Roman gods emerged with their status considerably enhanced. Venus seems originally to have been a relatively insignificant figure, but the connection with Aphrodite turned her into the hallowed goddess of love. In contrast, the Greek Ares was magnified by his association with Mars, for the Roman deity enjoyed a prestige befitting the war god of a martial people.

Inspired by the wealth of material suddenly opened up to them, Roman poets began retelling the Greek tales in Latin, substituting the Roman names for the gods. Although they frequently elaborated on the stories, they rarely invented material from scratch. To their audience, the myths seemed both ancient and exotic, and they acquired a new lease of life. It became fashionable for Romans to trace the origins of cities and dynasties back to a Greek or Trojan origin. Probably the best-known instance of this custom occurs in Virgil's epic, the *Aeneid*, which ascribes the origin of Rome itself to the activities of the displaced

15

Trojan, Aeneas, who first made his appearance as a character in Homer's *Iliad*.

As this kind of historical rewriting suggests, poets felt free to take considerable liberties in their handling of the tales. Sometimes Greek gods ended up being converted into Roman heroes. Such cavalier treatment paved the way for the time from the first century CE on when Roman propagandists would find it politically convenient

The *Aeneid*, written in the 1st century CE, followed in the epic tradition of the *Iliad* and the *Odyssey*. Virgil, its author, is shown with two muses in this 3rd-century CE Roman mosaic.

and expedient to bestow divine status on their living emperors.

Yet for all its borrowings from Greece, Roman religion remained a separate entity, with its own distinct atmosphere and identity. Its roots lay in the belief that all nature was full of *numina*—spirits that could also influence human destiny. The purpose of ritual was to placate these pervasive presences, which were expected in return to show favor to the worshipper.

While Greek religion was a civic faith, Roman worship had domestic roots in the farms and estates of the city's agricultural hinterland. Even though in time the faith took on all the trappings of state ceremony and ritual, it continued to have a strong presence in the home, where the deities known as *lares* and *penates* were honored in the hope that they would guarantee harmony and plenty. Significantly Vesta, the Roman goddess of the hearth, had a prominence in the nation's cults that her Greek equivalent Hestia never attained, while Janus, the double-faced god of the threshhold who kept evil out of the home, had no parallel at all in Hellenic religion.

In this family-oriented worship, the head of each household was the principal intermediary with the gods. He—for it was almost always a man—regularly took part in religious festivals that were held throughout the year. These included the Cerealia in honor of Ceres, an agricultural goddess; the late-summer festival dedicated to Consus and Ops, deities of the harvest; and the Saturnalia, held in December to honor Saturn. He also had to protect his family from the possibly malevolent influence of the spirits of the dead, calling on the help of the family *manes*, the shades of deceased ancestors, to do so.

As Rome's dominion grew, the state increasingly took on a religious function. While there were kings, the monarch assumed the role of householder for the nation as a whole. To help him in the task, a priesthood evolved, with the *pontifex maximus*, or chief priest, taking overall responsibility for the regulation of the constant round of festivals that punctuated the Roman, like the Greek, year. When the monarchy was overthrown in the sixth century BCE and a republic instituted, this officer continued to oversee religious affairs, which remained much as they had been under the previous regime.

Militarily, Roman expansion continued after Octavian won the fourteen-year civil war that followed Julius Caesar's assassination in 44 BCE and chose to rule alone as the first of the Roman emperors. The Empire saw Rome's power stretched to new frontiers. At its peak around 200 CE, Roman rule, and with it the cult of the classical gods, reached all the way from Scotland to the sands of Arabia, and from the Straits of Gibraltar to the Euphrates River.

Yet geographical dispersion went along with a dilution of the gods' power over peoples' hearts and minds. Gradually the classical myths lost the religious force they had once had, when they were accepted as true by the great body of the Greek population. The Roman attitude to the stories was both more sophisticated and more frivolous. Deprived of their original authority, the tales were fair game for poets like Ovid to embroider at will. By then they had left the field of religion for that of imaginative literature.

Eventually new faiths arose to fill the vacuum left by the decline of the old religion. The conversion of the Emperor Constantine to Christianity in 313 CE effectively outlawed the classical gods. For a millennium or more their worship had been an affair of state and a social necessity. Now it was proscribed as paganism, and the myths were criticized by Christian theologians for their immorality and lascivious invention.

When the last vestiges of the Western Empire collapsed and classical civilization was dismantled as invading peoples with their own gods swept across many of the lands the Roman legions had controlled, the fate of the Greek and Roman deities might have seemed to be well and truly sealed. Yet in spite of everything the memory of them was never entirely lost. They owed their survival to the poets and to the influence exercised on Christian writers by classical symbolism, literature, and art. The old tales were so deeply embedded in the corpus of classical culture that wherever shards of the shattered Graeco-Roman world survived, the names of Zeus and Jupiter, Aphrodite and Apollo lived on.

17

THE OLYMPIC GAMES

The original Olympic Games had a deeply religious aspect. Founded in 776 BCE at Zeus's sanctuary at Olympia, they brought the Greek world together to celebrate physical achievement in honor of the greatest of the gods. Athletes competed in a variety of events, including races over different distances, discus- and javelin-throwing, horse and chariot contests, boxing, and wrestling. Visitors who came to watch the sporting contests also took part in ceremonies and sacrifices in honor of Zeus.

Right: A 5th-century BCE statuette by the sculptor Myron depicts an athlete preparing to throw a discus. Contestants competed naked with oil rubbed into their skin to protect their pores against dirt.

Above: The bronze head of a wrestler, sculpted by an unknown Etruscan artist in the 3rd century BCE, shows the leather cap contestants wore to prevent opponents from grabbing them by their hair.

Right: The inscription on this bronze discus reveals that it was used by an athlete named Exoidas in a 6th-century BCE Olympic competition. Discus- and javelin-throwing are the oldest of all Olympic field events.

Above: Remnants of columns are all that survive to mark the original site of the Palaestra, the elaborate training center for boxers and wrestlers. It was added to the Olympic complex in the 3rd century BCE.

Above: The painting on this vase dated *c.* 530 BCE shows wrestlers locked in combat. This event, known as the *pankration*, had liberal rules: kicking was permitted and contestants were sometimes fatally injured.

Left: A 470 BCE vase commemorating the Games shows runners reaching the turning post in a long-distance race. The original Olympic track events were equivalent to our modern 100, 200 and 5,000 meters.

THE ORIGINS OF
THE WORLD

The Greeks and Romans did not have one authoritative version of the story of creation. Rather, countless, often contradictory, stories existed to explain the origin of the world that they knew, of the gods that they worshipped, and even their own beginnings. Ancient mythographers were comfortable with this profusion of tales, and storytellers and writers produced their own versions over the centuries. Many of these have been lost, and the earliest extant accounts are in the works attributed to the poets Homer and Hesiod.

Left: **Hecate, goddess of witchcraft (center), battles against a Giant in this sculpture dating from 180 BCE, which once decorated an altar in honor of Zeus.**

The tumultuous history of civilization in the Mediterranean helps to explain the abundance of creation myths. The Greek and Roman cultures both developed as syntheses of many different traditions, as successive waves of invaders imposed their own belief systems and traditions upon the native civilizations that they overran. Their mythological tales were combined with those of the people they conquered to produce the rich body of classical myth.

This background was reflected in the various accounts of creation. One thing that all the stories had in common was that they told of a long, eventful history. The ancient Greeks believed that both they themselves, and the gods they worshipped, were the products of generations of change and sometimes of violent revolution. Their sovereign deities, the Olympians, were not those who made the world, but rather, they represented the third generation of ruling divinities. Similarly, the race of humans of the classical period was—according to different sources—either the fourth or the fifth to live and breathe upon the Earth. Their earliest ancestors were thought of as living in a golden age, but since then there had been a gradual decline through a silver age into those of base metals. The Greeks, and later the Romans, were by no means confident that the process had ended, and believed that their generation, in the age of iron, might not last. In fact, *Works and Days*, the poem in which Hesiod gives his account of the creation of humankind, expresses his belief that his own race of humans is doomed to destruction because of its innate immorality.

Above: **A mischievous centaur, half man and half horse, has armed himself with a rock and a tree, in this painting from a 6th-century BCE vase. Centaurs and other magical creatures, both good and bad, were generated in the early phases of creation.**

21

Chaos and Its Offspring

The great mysteries of creation were explained by the Greeks and Romans in a number of different myths. The *Theogony*, written by Hesiod in the eighth century BCE, provided the earliest coherent account of how the cosmos, the gods, and mortals came into being. The poet also drew up a complete genealogy that traced the heritage of the Olympians back to the divine forces involved in the first acts of creation.

Hesiod was working from an oral tradition—a series of stories and songs that no longer exist. Other poets contemporary with him also composed accounts of the creation and genealogies of the gods. It is possible that the reason his version is the only one to have survived in its complete form is that it was the most comprehensive.

In Hesiod's account, the world evolved out of an enormous, shapeless darkness he called Chaos (meaning in Greek "a yawning void"). It was an abstract principle, the ultimate source of creation, and was not personified in any way as a primal god. Hesiod left open the question of how Chaos itself arose, because his aim was to provide a history of the gods, not of the universe: cosmogony was discussed only in terms of its effects on the intricate family tree he was creating. Nor did Hesiod explain how Chaos produced the five original elements: Gaia, the Earth; Tartarus, the Underworld located in the depths of the Earth; Erebus, the gloom of Tartarus; Eros, the force of love; and Nyx (Night), the power of darkness.

Throughout the ancient world, the night was acknowledged as an elemental force, since its mysterious darkness could conceal unknown evil and enemies. Its personification in myth as a goddess gave it a character and therefore made it a little less mysterious. Nevertheless, in Greek and Roman mythology, the goddess

Gaia, Mother Earth, is seated on her throne holding a newborn infant, a symbol of fertility, in this 5th-century BCE statue from Thebes.

Night was feared and respected even by her peers—Homer's *Iliad* describes her as having power over gods and men. She played a crucial role in most classical creation myths, and Hesiod's was no exception. In the *Theogony*, she was the first of the children of Chaos to give birth to other elements of the universe. Mating with Erebus, she bore Day and Aether, the pure upper atmosphere. Later she gave birth to many of the evils that cloud the lives of gods

and humans, including Doom, Death, Misery, Resentment, Deceit, and Strife; Strife herself went on to give birth to further afflictions, such as Murder, Carnage, Battle, and Lawlessness.

Gaia, the Earth, was next to produce offspring. On her own, she produced Uranus, the starry heavens, to cover her and to be a home for the gods who were to be created later. She also generated the Mountains (who had a divine

First Causes of Creation

Hesiod's story was only one version of the creation of the world. Many other influential myths of creation were also current.

Homer's account of creation respected the traditions of the seafaring folk for whom he originally composed his great epics. In the *Iliad* he told how all the gods and all living creatures began in Oceanus, the great sea that girdles the world.

Another early story described how a goddess was born spontaneously from Chaos. Finding nothing for her feet to rest on, she created the ocean and danced on its waves. The wind caused by her movements became the material from which she created a partner, a giant serpent. Taking the form of a dove, she laid a huge egg, which was fertilized by the serpent. Everything in the universe hatched from this primal egg.

In the creation myth of the Orphic cult, a major mystery religion, Chronos, the personification of Time, constructed an egg from which was born Phanes, the firstborn of

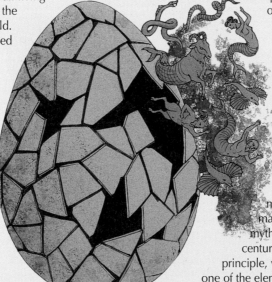

The cosmic egg is a source of creation in several different myths from ancient Greece and Rome.

the gods and the universal creator. Phanes took many forms, including Eros, the power of love. Eros was double-sexed, golden-winged, and four-headed. Night, his daughter, was also his consort and ultimately his successor. Everything on Earth and in the heavens resulted from their union.

While creation myths provided many people with sufficient answers to their questions about the origins of the universe, philosophers and scientists began their own investigations around the sixth century BCE. At first, scientific explanations reflected myth, as thinkers concentrated on defining the principle that first organized Chaos, a mystery that Hesiod and many other recorders of myth had left unsolved. For centuries, the organizing principle, whether conceived as one of the elements or as an intangible force, was thought to be divine. It was not until the late fifth century BCE that a scientist, Democritus, proposed a purely materialistic explanation of the existence of the world—one without a divine cause.

23

nature) and Pontus, the mythological personification of the sea, thereby bringing into existence the basic structure of the physical world.

Hesiod described Gaia, the Earth, as "broad-breasted, the secure foundation of all forever." Other classical poets called her the ultimate mother and nourisher, the source of all fertility in nature. Thus, she was not only the physical body of the Earth but also its essence and power (just as her first children were at the same time divinities

and elements of the cosmos). Belief in Gaia may predate that of the Olympian gods: archaeological evidence suggests that a female Earth divinity was worshipped in the Mediterranean from the earliest times. In some parts of Greece, as well as in Rome, where she was known as Tellus, she continued to be revered after the establishment of a pantheon of newer gods. The Romans, for example, worshipped her as the source of all babies, and for this reason they always placed their newborn infants momentarily on the ground just after birth to acknowledge the power of Tellus and draw strength from her.

Hesiod's myth of the formation of the physical world reflected the early Greek concept of the shape of the Earth. They believed that it was a flat disc rather than a sphere, and that their territory lay in the middle of that disc. Some identified its absolute center as Mount Olympus, the highest mountain of mainland Greece (see pages 42–3); others said it was the sacred oracular shrine of Delphi (see page 83). The land mass was completely encircled by a salt-water sea, known as Oceanus.

In myth, Oceanus, the child of Gaia and Uranus, was portrayed as a stream that always flowed smoothly, unaffected by storms or wind, and as the source of all other rivers. The idea that the Earth was a sphere first arose in the fourth century BCE, but even then the belief in an all-encircling Oceanus persisted, neither proved nor disproved by early seafaring explorers who attempted to circumnavigate the disc.

On this 6th- or 5th-century BCE Greek vase, Gaia (*center*) is shown emerging from the Earth and presenting an infant to Athena, as Zeus (*left*) looks on. Among the Greeks and the Romans, Gaia was revered as the source of newborn babies.

The Children of the Earth and Heavens

Although Uranus was born from Gaia, and so in one sense was her "son," he was not secondary to her. He was seen as her equal partner, consort, and husband. The union between Gaia and Uranus was a sacred marriage that brought together Earth and Heavens, joining a fertility goddess with a sky god.

The union between Gaia and Uranus was not viewed as improper in any way, despite the fact that Gaia was Uranus's mother. Two of their children would also marry each other, as would two of their grandchildren. With these marriages began a tradition that gods could break the taboo of incest, which for humans was inviolable.

Gaia and Uranus had numerous children, of whom many were monstrous in form and character. Their firstborn were the three Hecatonchires (the Hundred-handed)—male monsters with a semi-human form, but with one hundred arms and fifty heads each. Next came three more children, the one-eyed Cyclopes, named Arges (Bright), Brontes (Thunder), and Steropes (Lightning). They were strong and wild like their hundred-handed brothers. But they were also skilful stone-workers, believed to be the builders of the ancient, massive walls of Mycenae and the nearby fortress of Tiryns on the Peloponnese. Later Gaia, on her own or by various lovers, bore many other children. Most of these were also monsters, but not all. For example, one of her daughters was the lovely wood nymph Daphne (see page 131).

The most famous children of Uranus and Gaia were the twelve Titans, six sons and six daughters, who became the first gods: Oceanus, god of the seas (distinct from the geographical Oceanus), and his sister and mate, Tethys; Hyperion, a sun god, and his sister and mate Theia; Themis and Rhea, both Earth goddesses; Mnemosyne, the goddess of memory; Iapetus, Coeus, Crius, and Phoebe, whose specific functions are no longer known; and

Tellus, the Roman version of Gaia, is shown surrounded by her children on this relief panel from the Altar of Peace, commissioned by the emperor Augustus in 13 BCE.

Cronus, the youngest, boldest, and craftiest of the family, who hated his father and was to replace him as supreme god.

The Titans appeared early in the development of mythology in the eastern Mediterranean and in parts of Asia Minor. Most personified natural forces; Mnemosyne was an exception in being a personification of a human attribute, memory, and was a late addition to the pantheon. Although the generation of gods they produced, the Olympians, were to become more influential than them in Greek and Roman religion, the stories of the Titans

25

had a great significance. Many common themes of classical mythology derive from the stories told about them: notably the idea of a family of gods; of divine intermarriage, often within the same kinship group; and of power-sharing coexisting with competition for power.

The characters of the Titans, their children and the other monsters and divinities from this stage of creation are not as carefully delineated as those of the Olympians and other later gods. The few tales involving them usually serve to explain the nature of the physical world or the origins of the dominant generation of gods. This is true, for example, of Atlas, whose myths explain important aspects of geography and cosmology. Son of the Titan Iapetus and of Asia, a daughter of Oceanus, he was condemned in perpetuity to hold up the sky and prevent it from falling to the Earth, as a punishment for taking the Titans' side in a war between them and the Olympians (see page 34). According to one account, the range of mountains in northwest Africa that carries his name was created when he was turned to stone so that he would be strong enough to bear this oppressive burden. But despite his crucial responsibility for maintaining the position of the Earth, Atlas remains a one-dimensional figure in Greek myth, lacking any detailed characterization.

Mountains and Volcanoes

Behind the narrow strip of fertile land bordering the Greek coastline rise the mountains of the mainland. To people living near the coast who were dependent on the sea, these mountain ranges must have seemed an alien territory, the domain of gods and strange creatures.

For the ancient Greeks, mountains were powerful, magical places. They were full of mysterious caves, fissures, sudden springs, and river sources, and their summits were often concealed by clouds, mists and snow. In myth, they were the homes of gods, heroes, and monsters. Some myths explained the origins of specific peaks, including Atlas, Olympus, and Parnassus.

The volcanoes of the Mediterranean were an even greater source of wonder and apprehension. In addition to Etna and Vesuvius, which have erupted in modern times, many others, now quiescent, were still active during the classical period. The eruption of Thera (Santorini) in 1400 BCE, for example, devastated a thriving culture on that island. Many stories explained the violent behavior of active volcanoes. Etna was said to be the prison of a destructive monster, Typhon (see page 35), or the noisy workshop of Hephaestus, the divine smith, and Vesuvius was the explosive battleground of the ancient gods.

Fiery lava flowing from Mount Vesuvius cuts a destructive path through nearby settlements.

The Castration of Uranus

The marriage of Gaia and Uranus was riven by conflict. Gaia loved her children deeply, but their father felt only jealous contempt for them, fearing that one of his sons would eventually depose him.

Uranus buried his children deep within the Earth, locking them up again inside their mother's body as soon as they were born. Gaia had to endure double pain: the heartbreak of losing her children and the physical pain of their confinement within her own form. The monstrous Hundred-handed were held in Tartarus, a place so deep in the Earth that it would take an anvil thrown from heaven nine days to land there. The Cyclopes were condemned to live inside the volcanic core of Mount Etna, where their savage roaring was said to cause its frequently thunderous eruptions.

Eventually Gaia was no longer able to bear either her own pain or the insult to her and her children. She appealed to her Titan sons to liberate them all from their father's tyranny, but they were frightened of Uranus and one by one they turned down the challenge. Only Cronus, the youngest, dared to take up his mother's cause.

Gaia made a sickle for Cronus out of a material so hard that only the gods could make weapons from it. She plotted with her son how to catch Uranus off-guard, and showed him where to lie in wait within her body. As night fell, Uranus spread himself over the Earth and lowered himself toward his wife. Cronus lashed out with his sickle, castrating his father.

Many important mythical characters were born from the splashes of Uranus's blood, including the Giants, who were to become bitter enemies of a later generation of gods (see pages 34–5), the Erinyes, the vengeful Furies who punished patricides and other wrong-doers (see page 107), and the Meliae, nymphs of ash trees. Uranus's severed parts landed in the sea, where the mingling of the waves with the sperm that was released created the foam that gave birth to Aphrodite, who was later to become the Olympian goddess of love (see pages 62–7).

Shorn of generative power by his own son, Uranus was utterly humiliated and took little part in subsequent tales. Cronus took his place as an all-powerful sky god and soon set about establishing his own dynasty. Gaia, however, did not fade into the background in the same way that Uranus did. Although some of her roles and functions were adopted by future consorts of the principal god, she herself continued to be worshipped, particularly in Greece where she was a giver of oracles, and she appears infrequently but importantly in many later stories, often as an advisor to the gods or as a surrogate mother to them.

This 3rd-century Roman statuette, found in a settlement in Tunisia, shows Saturn, the Roman god equivalent to Cronus who castrated Uranus, his father.

Sickles, such as this iron example, were used to harvest grain and corn in the Greek and Roman world.

Helius and Phaethon

The Titans and their offspring played a role in establishing the natural order on Earth. Helius, the son of the Titan sun god Hyperion and his partner Theia, drove the chariot of the sun across the sky.

Helius steers the solar chariot from east to west in a 5th-century BCE Greek vase painting. The young boys leaping before him represent the stars fading in the light of day.

Phaethon was the son of Helius. His friends often teased him, saying that he could not be the son of a god, and even though his mother swore that it was true, the boy was not reassured. His mother finally advised him to visit his father Helius and ask him directly.

Phaethon traveled to Helius's magnificent palace to find out the truth. At first the boy could not approach his father because he was dazzled by the solar rays the god wore on his head. Putting the rays aside, Helius greeted his son with great affection and rashly promised to give the boy anything he wanted. Phaethon immediately asked to drive the chariot of the sun for one day.

Although Helius tried desperately to dissuade him, Phaethon was insistent, and Helius was bound by the promise he had made. He coated his son's face in an oil to protect his skin against the heat of the solar rays and tried to teach him the correct way to drive the chariot, but Phaethon was too impatient to listen.

The boy set out boldly, but as the horses rose into the sky they sensed their driver's inexperience and bolted downward. The terrified boy could not control the chariot and the horses drew the vehicle ever lower, searing much of the Earth with the sun's heat. The Nubian desert, once a fertile land, never recovered from this event, and the peoples of the south were so badly scorched that their skins turned black.

Seeing that the Earth risked total destruction, the gods blasted Phaethon, whose body crashed to Earth in flames. To save other lands from devastation, the gods cooled the heat of the solar chariot with a drenching cloudburst.

The Birth of Zeus

After defeating Uranus, Cronus became supreme ruler of the Titans. However, like his father, he feared being overthrown by a younger generation. Although he did his best to prevent this from happening, his children proved to be too clever for him.

The Greeks and Romans had different conceptions of Cronus. To the Greeks, the Titans were savage and uncouth in comparison with the later generation of Olympian gods. Nonetheless, Cronus was believed by some to have ruled over a golden age for humans (see page 36), and when he ceased to reign as supreme god, he retired to the Islands of the Blessed, a paradise somewhere in the far reaches of Oceanus, the great sea.

The Romans associated Cronus with Saturn, a god of agriculture, who possibly had native Italian roots or might have been an early import from the eastern Mediterranean. Like Cronus, Saturn was believed to have presided over a golden age in which humankind lived safely and peacefully. Always anxious to trace their own ancestry back to the gods, the Romans also devised a story that he was the first king of Latium and, through his son Picus, an ancestor of the Roman kings.

Both the Greeks and Romans agreed that Cronus was proud and confident. After the defeat of Uranus, he refused to bow to Gaia's wishes and release either the Hundred-handed or the Cyclopes from their prisons deep within the Earth—the injustice that had led her to promote Cronus over and above her husband in the first place. According to a slightly different version of the myth, he allowed Gaia to release them, but almost immediately reimprisoned them.

Cronus then married his sister Rhea, repeating the pattern of a male sky god marrying a mother goddess who represented the Earth and fertility. The other Titans also married each other, and six divine couples ruled the world together.

Cronus and Rhea had six children: Demeter, Hera, Hades, Poseidon, Hestia, and Zeus. However, Cronus had been warned by Gaia and

Rhea hands Cronus a stone wrapped in swaddling blankets in place of the infant Zeus, thereby saving the baby's life (see page 30), in a Roman marble relief dating from the 1st century BCE.

the wounded Uranus that he was fated to be supplanted by his son, just as he had deposed his father. Heeding this warning and hoping to cheat destiny, he ate all of his children at birth. In another version of the myth, his brothers allowed him to marry Rhea and act as supreme ruler on condition that he should not have any sons who could threaten his power and thus the security of the other Titans.

29

Zeus was sometimes said to have been raised on Mount Dicte on Crete. The mountainous interior of the island was sparsely populated in classical times and seemed to hold many mysteries.

Rhea, like her mother Gaia before her, was anguished by this destruction of her children, and she and Gaia conspired to protect her last baby. As soon as her son Zeus was born, Gaia carried him away to safety, while Rhea wrapped a stone in swaddling blankets and took it to Cronus, who swallowed the stone in place of the baby.

Gaia hid the infant god in a cave, usually believed to be on Mount Dicte on Crete, although Attica also claimed this honor. Here he was nursed by Amaltheia, who was both a goat and a nymph, and he was fed on her milk and on honey. Zeus later rewarded her faithful service by installing her in the heavens as the constellation Capricorn, the goat.

According to one myth, Rhea was concerned that her husband would find out about the child if he were to cry, and ordered a group of men to dance constantly around the cave entrance, singing loudly and clashing their spears and shields together to drown any sound the baby might make. These were the Curetes—mysterious, semi-divine young men noted for their noisy dances, who were mentioned frequently in Greek poetry. Scholars believe that they were mythical counterparts to the young Cretans who performed armed dances in rituals that honored their local version of Zeus.

Little is known about Zeus's education and upbringing on Crete. Some stories told that he was taught by Pan, half-man, half-goat and the god of the woodlands; others said that he grew up with the shepherds of Mount Ida. However, by the time Zeus came of age, he had learned of his mother's suffering, the destruction of his brothers and sisters, and Cronus's attempt to destroy him. He vowed that he would take his revenge.

Zeus's first wife was Metis, a sea nymph famous for her wisdom and cunning, who was later to become the mother of Athena (see page 70). Zeus persuaded her to administer an emetic to Cronus, which made him regurgitate Rhea's stone, followed by all the children he had swallowed earlier. The stone he had mistaken for Zeus was sometimes said to have been preserved at the oracular sanctuary at Delphi (see page 83). His brothers and sisters, grateful for their new-found liberty, immediately joined Zeus in an attempt to overthrow their father, and with him the entire race of the Titans.

Cybele, the Mother Goddess

Cybele was an Eastern fertility goddess whose cult was incorporated into Greek and Roman religion. She was often identified with Rhea, the Titaness and mother of Zeus.

According to the mythology, Cybele had once fallen passionately in love with a beautiful young man called Attis. She appointed him a priest of her temple at Pessinus in Phrygia (Anatolia). As priest, he was bound by an oath of chastity, but he broke this promise for love of the nymph Sagaris, whom he planned to marry. In her anger and jealousy, Cybele drove him insane so that he castrated himself and died.

A religious ritual developed around this narrative. The priests of Cybele were voluntary eunuchs known as *galli*. At the goddess's festivals they performed ritual dances in which they pretended to be mad—howling, shrieking, moaning, banging drums, and brandishing spears and shields. Because Cybele was often associated with Rhea, Zeus's mother, there appears to have been a connection between this curious ritual and the mythological dances of the Curetes who had protected Rhea's baby, the infant Zeus.

Cybele was more central to the Romans than she was to the Greeks. Inspired by the Sybilline Books, the Roman sacred prophetic literature, envoys brought the statue of Cybele from the temple at Pessinus to Rome in 204–205 CE. The goddess's public standing was enhanced by a legend about the statue's arrival. The ship carrying it became stuck on a mud shoal in the Tiber River, and no amount of effort could refloat it. At the same time, one of the Vestal Virgins (see page 105), named Claudia, was defending herself against claims that she had broken her sacred vow of chastity. She offered a test of her virtue: if she were still a virgin, Cybele would enable her to free the ship. She took her girdle, placed it around the prow, and effortlessly pulled the ship off the mud.

Cybele was usually represented as an imposing woman with a towering crown, riding in a chariot drawn by lions. Sometimes she was depicted with many breasts, or with two lion cubs held under her arms. Attis was often shown standing by her side, or following behind her.

A 4th-century BCE Greek carving shows Cybele, seated with a lion cub by her side, with Persephone, the daughter of Demeter. In Rome, Cybele was associated with Rhea, Zeus's mother.

The Battles of the Gods

Victory over his father did not come as easily to Zeus as it had to Cronus. Having rejected his son's claim to supremacy, Cronus called the other Titans and their children to his aid. Thus began the Titanomachy, a terrible war that would last for ten years. To the ancient Greeks, Hesiod's description of the battle would have seemed very real because of his reference to actual geographical features. Zeus and his siblings based themselves on Mount Olympus, in northern Greece, and his father and his allies established themselves to the south on Mount Othrys.

In his fight to defeat his son, Cronus could rely on most of his brothers and sisters, who were reluctant to lose what power they had under his leadership. Many of them had also produced powerful children, who were prepared to come to the aid of their uncle. Zeus and his siblings found themselves severely outnumbered.

Zeus then made a bold decision: he set free the Cyclopes, who had been imprisoned by Uranus, on the condition that they would make weapons for the Olympians. They accepted the offer, and made a helmet of darkness (or invisibility) for Hades, the great trident (a three-pronged fork) for Poseidon, and finally the thunderbolts that became both the instruments and symbol of Zeus's power. Next he released the Hundred-handed from Tartarus. They would prove to be powerful allies, because their hundred hands could hurl massive stones with great accuracy. These two moves also gained for Zeus the allegiance of Gaia, who had long been desperate to free her children.

Gaia urged the Titans to accept the rule of Zeus and depose Cronus peacefully. The wisest of her children agreed to do so, but most of them continued to support their brother. The Titans appointed Atlas, a son of Iapetus, as their military commander, and under his leadership a full-scale

The violence of the divine wars is captured in this altar to Zeus from a temple in Pergamon, *c.* 180 BCE. It shows a hound in Zeus's service killing a Giant.

Benevolent Monsters

In addition to the Titans and the Giants, the early period of creation produced many semi-human figures, not all of whom were vicious—some were even forces for good.

Pan, a god of the forests who introduced music to the world, was part goat and part human (see page 101). In most stories, he is considered the son of either Apollo or Hermes and a female nature spirit or nymph. The satyrs who accompanied Pan were endowed with similar animal features. They sometimes ran wild but at the same time they presented a joyous image of the creative life-force in their ecstatic dancing and pipe-playing.

Pegasus, the entrancing winged horse, had monstrous origins. He was born from the neck of the snake-haired Gorgon, Medusa, when the hero Perseus cut her head off. His father was Poseidon, who had slept with Medusa before she was transformed into a Gorgon (see page 125). Pegasus at first lived wild with the Muses on Mount Helicon in Greece. He was later tamed by Bellerophon, who rode the winged steed during his adventures. When the hero became arrogant enough to believe that he, a mortal, could reach Mount Olympus, Zeus caused Pegasus to rear up, throwing Bellerophon back down to Earth. The winged stallion then became the bearer of Zeus's thunderbolts. For his faithful service, Zeus honored Pegasus with a constellation.

The most famous benevolent monster was Chiron, a child of Cronus and the nymph Philyra, who was born a centaur, with the head and torso of a man and the body and legs of a horse. Although most centaurs were wild and cruel, Chiron grew up to be the wisest teacher in the world, and many of the heroes and the younger gods, including Asclepius, the son of Apollo and a renowned healer (see page 85), were sent to him for their education in music, medicine, and the arts. When Heracles wounded him accidentally, he suffered such agonies that he begged the gods to relieve him of his immortality and let him die peacefully. Although the request was unprecedented, Zeus agreed. After his death, Chiron was honored with a place in the heavens, in the constellation Sagittarius.

Centaurs cavort in this idyllic scene from a late Roman mosaic.

war broke out. At first the immense power of the thunderbolts seemed to give the Olympians an advantage, but Atlas rallied the Titans and their allies into a long resistance.

Eventually, Zeus's side began to regain the upper hand, and the Titans were besieged on Mount Othrys. The three brothers, Zeus, Hades, and Poseidon, held a war council, and a plot was laid. First, Hades crept unseen into Cronus's presence and stole his weapons. Then Poseidon began to threaten Cronus with the trident, while Zeus blasted him with his thunderbolts. Immediately the Hundred-handed started to rain rocks upon the remaining Titans.

This sudden combined attack led to total victory for Zeus's forces. Most of the Titans were hurled down into Tartarus, where they were guarded in perpetuity by the Hundred-handed. Atlas, as their military leader, was allotted a harsher punishment: he had to support the heavens on his shoulders for eternity (see page 26). Accounts differ as to whether Cronus was sent to be imprisoned in Tartarus or allowed to take up a dignified exile in the Islands of the Blessed. Some tales maintain that once Zeus had established his supremacy, he relented and pardoned all the Titans, leaving Atlas alone to bear his punishment.

The story of the Titanomachy reflects contemporary attitudes toward warfare. The ancient Greeks were themselves continually engaged in wars, between one city-state and another or against foreign enemies such as the Persians, and they valued courage and military skill highly. At the same time, they were suspicious of bloodlust and a mindless enthusiasm for destruction. Their mythical heroes were often those who used guile or knowledge, rather than sheer physical strength, to achieve their ends.

This theme emerges clearly in the tale of the battle of the Olympians against the Titans. Success for the young gods depended on cooperation and careful planning, while the cruder Titans were defeated, despite their greater strength.

Zeus had two more contests to face before he could confidently assert his authority over the world. The first was the Gigantomachy, the war against the Giants, which was one of the most popular myths in ancient Greece.

A centaur battles against a Lapith, a mythical inhabitant of Thessaly, on one of the metopes (carved panels) from the Parthenon, *c.* 440 BCE.

The Dark Spirits

During the violent wars of the gods, in these earliest times, many dark forces were created. Some of them survived the conflicts and continued to haunt and endanger humanity.

The Gorgons, three sisters with hideous round faces and snakes instead of hair, had the ability to turn any man who looked upon them into stone. The sisters of the Gorgons were the Graeae, who symbolized old age. At first they were conceived of as women who were born old and white-haired. In later tradition, they became hideous hags, grey-haired from birth, who shared only one tooth and one eye.

Echidna, described by Hesiod as an "impossible monster," was a beautiful woman from the waist up, and below a hideous serpent. She gave birth to a

A detail from a 5th-century BCE Greek vase showing the head of a Gorgon.

series of unnatural offspring by mating with Typhon, the monster created by Gaia to fight against Zeus. Echidna's children included Cerberus, the three-headed hound of hell, who guarded the gates of the Underworld. Foam from his mouth generated poisonous plants. The fire-breathing Chimaera was part lion, part serpent, and part goat. The Sphinx, which had the head of a woman and the body of a lion, preyed viciously on the inhabitants of Thebes; similarly the Nemean Lion was reputed to harass and attack the hapless people of the town of Nemea.

Although Gaia had sided with Zeus, her grandson, against her own children, she became infuriated by his high-handed ways and turned to the Giants to help her defeat him. There are two accounts of their origins: some claimed that the Giants already existed, conceived from the blood of Uranus's castration (see page 27); other versions said that Gaia only generated these offspring after the defeat of the Titans.

Encouraged by Gaia, the Giants hurled huge rocks and burning oak trees at the heavens. Fighting against them, Zeus, Poseidon, and Hades were now assisted by their children, and Ares, Hermes, Apollo, Artemis, and Athena all played crucial parts in the war. The gods learned through an oracle that, although they would be able to injure the Giants, it would take a mortal to issue the death-blow. Athena, with Zeus's permission, enlisted Heracles, a half-human half-god known for his strength, to the gods' side. With his help, the Olympians were finally able to kill the Giants.

However, Gaia's anger did not abate after Zeus and the Olympians had defeated her champions. She immediately generated an even more formidable monster, Typhon, who had a hundred dragon heads, coiling serpents for legs and hundreds of hands. Zeus took on this terrifying adversary in one-to-one combat. At one point Typhon managed to slice out Zeus's sinews from his hands and feet and hide them, but they were found by Hermes who refitted them. Restored to strength, Zeus returned to the fray. Gradually he was able to drive Typhon out of Greece, finally crushing him under volcanic Mount Etna.

This proved to be Gaia's final effort against Zeus. She now acknowledged his supremacy, and he and his clan at last returned victorious to their home on Olympus.

The Ages of Humankind

Just as there are a variety of myths explaining the beginning of the world and the origins of the gods, so there are a number of different traditions about the creation of humanity. The myths even differed as to which god, Cronus or Zeus, was responsible.

Hesiod, the eighth-century BCE Greek poet who compiled the most coherent genealogy of the gods (see page 22), also told the story of the birth of humanity in a poem called *Works and Days*. In this he described the creation by the gods of five different races of human beings who lived one after the other.

In the earliest times, when Cronus, father of Zeus, was the supreme god, there was a golden race of mortals. The men of gold lived free from all cares and worries, eternally young. Hesiod was not clear about what happened to this blessed race, saying only that the Earth covered it over, burying it, and that the souls of the golden ones survived as guardian spirits. Other writers suggested that the terrible wars of the gods led to their destruction. A later Roman version of this myth maintained that the people of the golden age lived in Italy where they were ruled over by Saturn, the god whom the Romans associated with Cronus. This version was written for patriotic motives to glorify Saturn, from whom the Romans traced their ancestry.

Hesiod claimed that after the golden race vanished from the Earth, Zeus created a race of silver. These mortals were inferior to those created by his father, and their lives were less idyllic. The seasons divided the year up, and the cold and rain of winter obliged people to live in caves. The Earth no longer provided them with food spontaneously. This race turned out to be childish and irresponsible. They refused to offer sacrifices and treated the gods who came among them with contempt. In the end they so infuriated the Olympians that they were all destroyed.

Zeus then decided to experiment with a race of bronze, made from ash trees and endowed with

In this early Roman relief, Saturn is shown holding a knife and standing before an animal that is about to be sacrificed. Originally an Italian agricultural god, Saturn came to be identified with the Greek deity Cronus. He ruled over the age of gold.

hearts of stone. They were highly skilled in bronzework, arming themselves and building their houses out of the metal. However, the men of this race were terrifying and warlike—they were so addicted to fighting and combat that they soon annihilated each other and dwelled thereafter in the Underworld.

The heroic age followed this disastrous experiment. While the inclusion of a heroic age

Prometheus, Friend of Humankind

Not all the classical creation myths identified Zeus as the creator of humankind. One tradition maintained that Prometheus, a Titan, created the human race and then remained its advocate in the face of the supreme god's hostility.

During the war between the Titans and Olympians, some of the Titans' children sided with Zeus and his brothers. One of these was Prometheus, whose name in Greek means "forethought" and who was able to foresee that Zeus would be victorious. To reward him for his faithful service, Zeus gave him the task of creating life for the Earth. After he had made the animals with Zeus's aproval, Prometheus sculpted clay figures, modelled on the gods, which could stand upright. Pleased with his work, he gave these figures life, but this time without seeking Zeus's permission.

Because of this insult, Zeus never cared for humans. Only Prometheus's intervention eased their lives. For example, it was his guile that won for them the better portion of the meat from sacrificial animals. He hid the choice cuts of meat under an animal's stomach, then wrapped the bones and entrails in delicious-looking fat, before inviting Zeus to choose the gods' portion. Zeus was deceived, and the people had meat to eat. Ever after human celebrants at sacrifices received the tastiest parts of the animal (see page 43).

Then Prometheus stole fire from heaven and gave it to his human creations. Zeus, outraged, ordered that the thief should be tied to a rock for eternity. Each day an eagle came and ate out his liver, which grew again the following night.

To punish humankind for Prometheus's gifts, Zeus designed a beautiful but wicked novelty—a woman, Pandora, who was as foolish as she was alluring. Zeus sent her to Earth carrying a pot that she was ordered never to open. The men,

enchanted by her charm, welcomed her among them. But soon, stupidly, she opened the secret vessel, as Zeus knew she would, and out of it flew the miseries that afflict humanity, such as war, famine, and sin. Only hope, ever deceptive, remained in the pot, a slight comfort.

Prometheus himself was released from his torture after thirty thousand years. It was said that he possessed a secret so important that Zeus gave him his freedom in exchange for the knowledge. This secret was that Zeus could only be overthrown by a child he fathered by the nymph Thetis, and with this warning, Zeus was able to avoid the fate that had befallen his father and his grandfather.

Prometheus is shown bound to a tree rather than a rock in this detail from a 6th-century BCE bowl. His liver is being plucked out by an eagle as Atlas, his brother, looks on.

Deucalion and Pyrrha

The story of a destructive flood that leaves the Earth ready for repopulation is one of the most common myths in cultures all around the globe.

The idea of widespread human evil being punished by a global catastrophe is shared by many mythological traditions, including those of India, Native America, China, and Aboriginal Australia. Usually, a few righteous people are saved from the devastation, and they repopulate the world, passing on their knowledge, skills, and high moral standards. The biblical story of Noah and the ark is perhaps the best-known example of the story. It may reflect in part a Babylonian account of a catastrophic deluge, which also may have influenced the Greek tale of Deucalion and Pyrrha.

In this story, Zeus, disgusted by the wickedness of the people of the iron age, determined to destroy the human race. He decided to do so by means of a deluge that would inundate the Earth, drowning all the people. While he unleashed torrential rain, Poseidon stirred up the rivers and the seas and caused earthquakes. Nearly all the people on Earth died, either by drowning or from starvation.

Only two good and reverent individuals were saved: Deucalion, son of Prometheus and king of Pthia, and his wife Pyrrha. Warned of the flood by Prometheus, they had time to seek safety in a boat that was well provided with food. After nine days, the boat came to land on the peak of Mount Parnassus. Zeus, recognizing their virtue, let them live. The rains stopped, and the waters gradually fell. At length, the couple were able to descend the mountain to the sacred cave of Delphi.

Deucalion and Pyrrha were safe but sad, lonely, and purposeless in the empty world. They offered up prayers. From the cave the oracle spoke to them: "Throw your mother's bones over your shoulders."

This instruction at first dismayed the couple, because disrespect for the bones of an ancestor was among the worst of sacrileges. But suddenly Deucalion understood the oracle's puzzling command. The Earth was their mother, and the rocks around them were her bones. Picking up stones, he threw them over his shoulder, and Pyrrha followed suit. Each stone that Deucalion threw hit the ground and became a man, and each of Pyrrha's stones became a woman, until the world was peopled again.

disrupted the pattern of ages of metal, it allowed Hesiod to accommodate the epic tradition of the legendary heroes, considered his immediate predecessors. Hence the heroic age was a race of demi-gods, also created by Zeus—the men who were celebrated in the great heroic myths. When they died, many of these heroes were either placed in the heavens as constellations, became companions to the gods, or were granted a blissful existence in the Islands of the Blessed.

Finally, Zeus created the present age of human beings, the age of iron. This race was born to toil and was afflicted with all kinds of troubles by the gods. Hesiod believed that the race of iron was fated for destruction: it would be wiped out either by an act of Zeus or by warfare. The end would be near when babies began to be born white-haired and prematurely senile.

When, eight hundred years later, the Roman poet Ovid came to rewrite these myths in his great work, the *Metamorphoses*, he omitted the heroic age from his account. The tradition of the heroes was no longer as influential in his time as it had been in Hesiod's, and thus he wrote only of four ages of mankind rather than five. Nonetheless, the myth of the heroic age was not a significant strand in mythology, its importance being shown by the widespread religious practice of hero sacrifice. This had less in common with sacrifices to the Olympian gods than with those made to the chthonic deities (see page 10), in that the rites took place in the evening and involved the offering of a black animal. These sacrifices sought the goodwill of a person whose greatness while alive had gained him or her continued power after death. Sacrifices were offered to dead ancestors, but also to kings, soldiers, and even valiant enemies, because a bold enemy was also respected as a hero. Roman emperors based their claim to divinity in part on this tradition: the idea that men could be demi-gods, eternally powerful, gave the emperors a way in which to promote themselves from powerful mortals to incarnate gods during their own lifetimes.

Achilles, one of the mythical Greek heroes of the Trojan War, dies in the arms of his comrades. His story is memorably told in Homer's *Iliad*. The myths of the heroes were so influential in ancient Greece that Hesiod included a race of heroes in his account of the origins of mankind.

THE FIRST FAMILY OF OLYMPUS

In 66 CE, only two years after the great fire in Rome, the Emperor Nero left the capital to journey to Greece for the Olympic Games. The Roman Empire was facing a crisis because insurrection had escalated into war in Palestine, and the ruler's popularity had sunk to a new low. Yet Nero's main concern at the time was to become one of the victors at the world's most famous athletic contest, which had been celebrated for more than 1,000 years. By sharing in the glory of the event, he hoped to shore up his flagging reputation.

According to one legend, the games had been instituted by the Olympian god Zeus to celebrate his defeat of the Titans and his success in establishing himself and his family as the ruling deities. The great wars of the gods had ended and the children of Cronus and Rhea had introduced a new world order. In the future, there would be concord between Earth and Heaven; although the gods were powerful, they could also be caring, and would give help and support to humankind from their divine home on Olympus. This new reign of peace was hard-won, and it would therefore be all the more valued by both gods and mortals.

Olympia, the sacred shrine of Zeus, was, for the people of Greece and later of Rome, a symbol of the lasting authority and power of the supreme deity and his brothers and sisters. Although the games at first admitted only Greeks, by the time of Nero they were open to all men of honor, of any nationality, demonstrating that the Olympian gods were above local rivalries. To the people who joined in the celebrations, the Games represented a stable world order.

Nero—who, like other Roman emperors, claimed to trace his family line back to the Olympian gods and thus believed he was a direct descendent of Zeus and shared in his divinity—must have enjoyed this historic event. He was indeed declared a champion, although only after considerable manipulation of the rules, and, as was the right of all champions, he returned to Rome in state. He may even have gained some personal reassurance in those troubled times from the magnificence of the Olympian stadium and the long-lasting influence of the Olympian gods.

Hera, the wife of Zeus, was the goddess of marriage and of child-birth. In this 4th-century BCE terracotta bust, she is holding an egg, a symbol of fertility.

Opposite: This larger than life-size bronze statue, dating from c. 450 BCE, depicts either Zeus or Poseidon. It was found in the sea off the coast of Artemision, in northern Greece.

41

Olympus: Dwelling of the Gods

Once victorious, the children of Cronus and Rhea were free to establish their kingdom. In the myths, they made their home on Mount Olympus, the highest mountain in northern Greece, an isolated peak surrounded by beautiful countryside. Although the actual mountain is craggy and forbidding, life on the mythical peak was idyllic.

To the early Greek city-states, Mount Olympus had great strategic importance because it formed a key part of the natural defense against invaders from the north. The need for such a defense against a common enemy was an important source of solidarity between the city-states. They also shared a language and a belief in the same pantheon of gods, although they were governed independently and remained geographically separate. By establishing Mount Olympus as the home of these gods, the Greeks acknowledged its strategic and psychological significance. In addition, by giving the Olympians a common residence, they reinforced the concept of a family of divinities.

In their legends and their worship, the Greeks behaved as though the gods actually lived on Mount Olympus. At the same time, they were aware that this was not reality, and that the home of the gods was a remote place above the heavens. Nonetheless, it is in real locations that most of the episodes of classical myth unfold.

On the Olympus of the imagination, as on Earth, the sun would rise in the morning and set in the evening, but the weather was always clear and calm. The grand entrance made of clouds was guarded not by armed warriors or threatening animals, but by the Horae—three beautiful goddesses, also called the Seasons (the classical people of the Mediterranean recognized only spring, winter, and summer). The Horae kept track of which gods were abroad in the world, and welcomed them on their return.

Inside the realm of Olympus, each of the gods had a home of his or her own, designed in solid brass by Hephaestus, the divine smith (see pages 86–8). But the center of Olympian life was the

At its highest point, Mount Olympus rises 9,570 ft. (2,917 m). Its summit is known as "The Throne of Zeus." In mythology, the mountain was home to the Olympian gods; historically it played an important strategic role for the ancient Greeks, helping to protect their territory against invaders from the north.

palace of Zeus. All the gods would come to its great hall when summoned, and they feasted there nightly on ambrosia and nectar, their divine food and drink.

Life on Olympus was marked by beauty, ingenuity, and creativity. Hephaestus, with divine artistry, designed every sort of comfort for his fellow gods—the solid gold tables and chairs could even move themselves in and out of the great hall as occasion demanded. The gods' clothes were woven by Athena (see pages 72–3) and the Graces (see page 63).

Mortals were never permitted to enter the home of the gods, even in times of desperate need. Virtuous Greeks or Romans did not expect to go to Olympus when they died—they would go to the Elysian Fields (see pages 108, 110), deep in the Underworld, or to the Islands of the Blessed, situated at the far edge of the Earth, in Oceanus, the mythical sea.

Sacrifice

In addition to a common home, the Olympians shared one form of worship. The sacrifice of animals was a central part of religious observance honoring all the gods. The Greeks and Romans believed keenly in the principle of reciprocity: offerings to the gods were made to thank them for their favor and at the same time to bind them by honor to continue to extend their goodwill.

Some myths contain mentions of human sacrifice, mainly associated with the goddess Artemis (see page 81). However, it is not clear whether these reflect historical reality or are purely fictitious. By the time of Homer, it is clear that only animals were offered in sacrifice. Each god had a characteristic sacrificial animal. For example, bulls were sacred to Zeus, horses to Poseidon, and cows to Hera. It was essential that the sacrificial animal was in perfect condition—sacrificing a blemished or diseased animal was considered an insult to the god. The Romans most commonly sacrificed pigs, although sheep and oxen were also offered on important occasions. But only parts of the animal were presented to the god. In Greece the god received a burnt portion sometimes consisting just of the bones and the tail, while in Rome, the god's lot was the heart, liver, or kidneys. The rest of the meat was eaten by the priests and participants in the sacrificial rite.

Each sacrifice was accompanied by prayers and other practices, such as ritual washing and the offering of grain and hair. Sacrifices to the Olympian gods took place at dawn and to the chthonic deities (see page 10), such as Hades, at sunset. They were an essential part of festivals and competitions honoring the gods, but sacrifices could also be made at other times, often preceding, for example, important state occasions, battles, or the signing of treaties.

In Rome, sacrifice took on additional significance because of the belief in augury—seeking out omens and signs of the future. While the Greeks often consulted oracles to learn their future, the Romans preferred an elaborate system of examining the entrails of sacrificed animals before making any major political or personal decisions.

This detail from a red-figure vase, dating from the end of the 5th century BCE, shows the ritual slaughter of a deer in honor of the gods.

The First Couple: Zeus and Hera

After Cronus's sons defeated their father and his generation of gods, they divided the universe among themselves. Zeus took the heavens for his share. Formerly the leader of the rebellion against the older generation, he now assumed supremacy over gods and humankind. His consort, Hera, had an equally exalted position.

Zeus was the supreme god, the father figure of Mount Olympus who maintained order among the often quarrelsome Olympian gods. On Earth, Zeus was worshipped as the ultimate protector of state and family, and as the source of the most esteemed qualities, such as justice, hospitality, fair government, and the honoring of oaths. In sacrifices, he was offered the blood of goats, sheep, and especially white bulls—because bulls were the fiercest and most powerful animals known to the early Greeks, they were especially sacred to Zeus, the mightiest of the gods. Oak trees were also sacred to him. The Olympic Games, the athletic contest held regularly in Zeus's honor, was among the most important festivals in ancient Greece, and they continued throughout the Roman period (see pages 18–19). The four-year interval between the Games became the universal chronological reference point, much in the same way as decades are today.

In art, Zeus was often represented in great majesty, sitting on a gold or ivory throne, with his thunderbolts ready in one hand and a scepter in the other. His beard was long, and he was accompanied by a sacred eagle with its wings spread. One of the seven wonders of the ancient world was the 43-foot- (13 m) high statue to him that stood in his temple at Olympia, in the Peloponnese. Crafted by Phidias, the foremost Athenian sculptor, and completed c. 430 BCE, it was covered with gold, ivory, and precious metals.

Although he had the highest status among the gods, many of the stories told about Zeus present a less than admirable side to his nature. He was frequently angry, temperamental, and unreasonable, hurling his thunderbolts impetuously, tricking his friends and deceiving Hera. Above all, Zeus was highly amorous, and in his efforts to seduce, he knew no boundaries. In many tales, he assumed false shapes in order to beguile the women on whom he had set his eye. This was partly because mortals would die instantly upon seeing him in his full splendor; but Zeus also

Zeus stands ready for battle, holding his thunderbolt high, in a bronze statue dating from the 6th century BCE.

relied on deception to achieve his ends. For example, he disguised himself as Artemis in order to corrupt Callisto, one of the virgin nymphs who accompanied that chaste goddess; he came to Danae as a shower of gold, and to Aegina as a flame of fire. And, perhaps most famously of all, as a great white swan he raped Leda, wife of Tyndarus, king of Sparta, even though he knew she was pregnant.

As a great god, Zeus was extremely potent—he had such an enormous number of children, including gods, immortals, and humans, that it is impossible to give a full list of his offspring. Apart from the second generation of the Olympians, all of whom were his progeny, he was the father of many of the minor gods, including Hermes, the Fates, the Muses, the Seasons, and the Graces, and also of several key characters in the great stories of classical mythology, such as Persephone, whose mother Demeter was his sister. In addition, he was the father of a number of the heroes, including Heracles.

Zeus's promiscuity played a key role in the development of a unified mythology. The common religion of the Greek world was an amalgam of local traditions that combined over the centuries with belief systems introduced by invading tribes and other foreign influences. One of the easiest ways for early mythographers to incorporate a new tradition within the core body of myth was to identify imported deities with the Olympian gods. Sometimes, the Olympian would take on the attributes of the new god. For example, Zeus possesses traits of a sky god who was held sacred by the earliest Greek-speaking people in the second millennium BCE, as well as those of a Cretan sky god, confirming his close ties with the island. In other cases, the local god or goddess became a sexual conquest of one of the Olympian gods, most often Zeus.

Given the fact that he had overthrown his own father, Cronus, to become ruler of the world (just as Cronus had usurped Uranus), Zeus was understandably wary that he too was fated to be supplanted by his children. However, he was able

This temple to Hera, the wife of Zeus, was built in the Greek colony of Poseidonia, known to the Romans as Paestum, in southern Italy in the mid-6th century BCE. Its mighty columns have withstood the test of time. It stands next to an equally impressive temple to Poseidon that was built a century later.

to break the pattern because he was not only warned of the danger of overthrow but also took steps to avoid it. He restrained his lust for the Nereid Thetis, because she was fated to bear a son who would be mightier than his father. He also swallowed Metis, the Titan goddess of wisdom, after he made her pregnant, because it was prophesied that their offspring too would be powerful. He gave birth to their child, Athena, on his own, thus neutralizing the prophecy (see page 70).

Disloyal and even cruel to his wife and mistresses, he nonetheless honored his family. In this respect, he reflected classical society. Both Greek and Roman men esteemed family honor, and the Greek male social elite had no problem reconciling this with extramarital relationships involving both women and younger men. And although in the early days of the Roman republic morality was somewhat stricter, the emperors were notoriously less inhibited in their behavior—as though, once they started to think of themselves as representatives of Jupiter (the Roman Zeus), they felt free to emulate his habits.

45

Nothing so clearly shows the division between the public and the private roles of Zeus as his relationship with his wife, Hera. The couple were brother and sister, joined in a sacred marriage between a sky god and an earth goddess, just as Gaia and Uranus and Rhea and Cronus had been before them. They were brought together as a result of Zeus's sexual trickery. Charmed by his sister, Zeus disguised himself as a cuckoo and, feigning cold, snuggled himself to her breast, where she received him tenderly, becoming yet another victim of his amorous deceptions.

As Zeus's wife, Hera was queen of all the gods. Her worship was as widespread as his, and an ewe lamb and a sow were usually sacrificed to her on the first day of every month. She was the patroness of marriage and married women, punishing adultery severely and rewarding chastity and devotion. Like some of the other female

Olympians, she had a role as a protector of childbirth: the Milky Way is so called because it was created from milk that had spilled from her breasts when she was nursing the hero Heracles. Her milk could confer immortality. In Rome, where home and household were extremely important, her authority was even greater. In her Roman form of Juno, she was goddess of cleanliness and good order, as well as of power, empire, and riches. She could give or withhold prosperity and worldly success, and all the consuls were required to make a special sacrifice to her before they could take up office. Her representation in art reflects this high esteem. She is usually shown seated on a throne or driving a chariot drawn by peacocks, attended by Iris, goddess of the rainbow.

Despite her high status, her married life was chaotic. She was almost insanely jealous of her husband's mistresses, persecuting them unmercifully and punishing their offspring. Zeus retaliated with abuse and violence, once hanging her up in the great hall of Olympus for the other gods to laugh at. At one time she left him and went to live on Euboea, an island close to the east coast of mainland Greece. Zeus desperately wanted her back and finally effected a reconciliation, but their reunion did not last. Despite this endless cycle of infidelity and jealousy, however, the long-lasting bond of Zeus and Hera symbolized the significance and the strength of marriage in Greek and Roman culture.

This pattern of public dignity and private license, of immense divine power and squabbling pettiness, distinguishes the characters of all the gods of Greece and Rome. In terms of personality, their supreme deities are remarkably human—none of the gods is either totally good or totally bad, but like humankind, they combine both positive and negative traits. Zeus and Hera, the first couple of Olympus, were subject to the same emotional complexity as mortals.

In this 5th-century BCE terra-cotta, Zeus is accompanied by Ganymede, a mortal youth with whom he was enamored. The statue was found in Zeus's sanctuary at Olympia.

Europa and the Bull

Zeus was famous for his adventures, and many of the stories of classical mythology start with his seduction of a mortal woman. For example, the city of Thebes was said to have been founded as a result of Zeus's desire for Europa, daughter of the king of Phoenicia.

One day Princess Europa went with her friends to gather flowers in a meadow beside the ocean. The group of laughing girls in the hot sunshine was a charming sight, and most delightful of all was Europa herself. She was so appealing that Zeus could not resist her. But knowing everything, he was aware that she was as pure as she was beautiful, and that he would be able to seduce her only through subterfuge.

In the meadows where the girls played, a herd of handsome cows was grazing peacefully. They were the prize cattle of Europa's father, and the girls paid little attention to them. Then one of them noticed a new bull in the herd. They were curious, as young girls are, because the bull was more beautiful, stronger, and larger than any they had ever seen. The princess went up to the animal and, despite its strength and size, it turned out to be gentle and playful. Her companions told their parents later that they had plaited flower garlands for the bull and it had let them dress it up and pet it. "It was a game," they said, "just a game. It knelt down and she climbed on its back."

Hardly had Europa settled on the bull's broad shoulders than it charged down toward the shore with the girl clinging desperately to its horns. It galloped into the waves, and by the time Europa realized that this was no game, the bull was swimming; she was out of her depth and there was no alternative but to cling on tightly.

Only when they came ashore on the island of Crete did Zeus reveal to her his true identity. Europa was unable to resist him and eventually bore him three sons, Minos, Rhadamanthus, and Sarpedon (see page 110).

This 1st-century CE wall painting from Pompeii shows Europa, accompanied by her friends, sitting on the back of a magnificent bull, which was actually Zeus in disguise.

Back in Phoenicia her family continued to mourn their loss. Finally, Europa's brother Cadmus, feeling compelled to take action, set out and wandered over all the world seeking his lovely sister. But he never discovered where Zeus had hidden her. Unable to return home and face his father's profound grief, he built a new city in Greece: Thebes.

The Muses

*The nine Muses—immortal nymphs, nature spirits whose father
was Zeus—were the source of inspiration to poets, dramatists, and
musicians. They were precisely personified, each with her own
duties and her own symbolism.*

Although most personifications
of virtues or of natural phenomena were not given detailed characterizations, the Muses were an
exception. This was because it
was the religious duty of all
poets to acknowledge them as
the source of their creative
artistry. Over the centuries the
invocations to each became
more distinctive, and the Muses
developed their identities.

The Muses were the children
of Zeus and Mnemosyne, the
Titan goddess of memory. Each
of the Muses had individual
responsibilities, and together
they represented the complete
range of the classical arts.

Calliope was the muse of epic,
heroic poetry, ranked most
senior of all the arts. Clio represented history, the recounting of
which was considered an art in
the classical world. Euterpe was
the muse of lyric poetry and its
accompanying music. Thalia
inspired festivals as well as the
forms of pastoral and comic
poetry that evolved from the
sometimes riotous processions
that were a central part of many
of them. Melpomene, the muse
of tragedy, was always depicted
as being more solemn than the
others. Terpsichore influenced
dancing. Erato was the inspiration of tender or amorous

poetry; in Roman times she was
also associated with April, which
was seen as the month of lovers.
Polyhymnia's provinces were
song, the lyre and musical enter-
tainments. The ninth muse,
Urania, represented astronomy,
indicating the poetic and mythological importance of the stars
and planets.

The Muses were flower-
bedecked virgins who lived in
woods and beside fountains.
They were often shown dancing
in a circle, holding hands, to
suggest the intimate connection
between all the arts. Laurel
bushes were sacred to the
Muses, and winners of the great
festival competitions in poetry
and in drama were crowned
with wreaths made from these
plants. The laurel was also the
plant sacred to Apollo (see page
131), the Olympian patron of
song and the lyre who was associated with the Muses. For this
reason, he was sometimes
known as Apollo Musegetes, or
leader of the Muses.

**This detail from a carving decorating a
Roman sarcophagus dating from the 1st
century CE shows two of the Muses
accompanying a musician. Artists
throughout the classical world called
upon the Muses for creative inspiration.
They were invoked at the beginning of
poems and plays, and poets vied with
one another to be the most fulsome in
their praise of them.**

Poseidon, God of the Oceans

Poseidon received the oceans as his portion when the victorious Olympians divided the universe among themselves. The stories about him reflect the respect, love, and fear that the sea inspired in the Mediterranean world.

The sea was of great importance to the Greeks and Romans, because it was one of their principal means of transport and communication. Sea travel, however, was fraught with danger, so both cultures perceived Poseidon as a dangerous and often dark god. He was so significant that in some parts of the Mediterranean he was regarded as equal to Zeus. Myths arose drawing parallels between the stories of their births, explaining that Poseidon had also been protected by his mother,

A triumphant Poseidon, holding his trident aloft, is pulled by seahorses in his ocean-going chariot. A mosaic from the first half of the 3rd century CE, found in a house in modern-day Tunisia.

Rhea, as a newborn baby. Although Cronus, her partner, swallowed all of their children as they emerged from the womb, Rhea gave Cronus a rock to swallow in Zeus's place; some versions of the myth relate that she gave Cronus a foal to devour instead of Poseidon.

The myths about Poseidon and the rites of his worship reflect his fearsome power. On the one hand, he had more authority than any other god except Zeus, and controlled not only the oceans but all the rivers, streams, and fountains of the world. He was a god of great beauty and was often shown standing in a chariot made of a shell drawn by winged horses, holding aloft his three-pronged trident. In his magnificent palace under the sea, he was attended by dolphins and fish, and by the Nereids, fifty nymphs who lived on the seashore in caves or grottoes.

This image of Poseidon throwing his trident decorates a Greek coin, known as a *stater*. It was used in the colony of Poseidonia, which was dedicated to him (the town was called Paestum by the Romans), *c.* 500 BCE.

The darker side of Poseidon was represented by stories of his dangerous temper and jealous behavior. Soon after the defeat of the Titans, he decided that he had been unfairly treated by Zeus and attempted to stage a rebellion. The conspiracy was discovered and, as punishment, Poseidon was made to build the walls of Troy. Homer tells how he could cross the world in just three strides, causing the mountains to tremble; he was also the god of earthquakes and, in some accounts, of volcanoes.

Poseidon was often in conflict with the other gods. He became involved in a dispute with Apollo over control of the isthmus of Corinth: this was ultimately divided between the two gods. But his most famous quarrel was with Athena, Zeus's favorite daughter, with whom he contested the patronage of Athens (see page 71). He found himself in opposition with her again during the ten-year-long Trojan War, when she supported the Greeks and he the Trojans.

His worship could have declined under the Romans, who knew him as Neptune, because they were less dependent on seafaring than the Greeks. However, he was also linked with horses, which were important to the Roman military. Poseidon's association with horses may stem from an older, lost tradition in which he was not purely a marine god; his role as generator of earthquakes and volcanoes may also be related to this tradition. In many stories, he either created horses or made them appear, and in one tale he assumed the shape of a horse to seduce his sister, Demeter, who was disguised as a mare. Their offspring was Arion, a horse with two human feet who could run extraordinarily fast. Both the Greeks and the Romans honored Poseidon (Neptune) with major annual festivals: the Isthmian Games at Corinth and the Consualia in Rome. At this latter festival horses, saddled and decorated with flowers, were led through the city streets to Neptune's temple in the Forum. His sacrificial animals were bulls and horses.

Poseidon was regarded as being as lustful as his brother Zeus, and many of the myths about him are related to his conquests. He was married to Amphitrite, even though she had taken a vow of celibacy. They had one son, Triton, who became a powerful sea god himself. Despite his marriage Poseidon was, like Zeus, continually engaged in amorous escapades. He often appeared to the objects of his desire in different forms. For example, after he rescued the princess Theophane, who was distressed because she was pursued by too many suitors, he turned her into a ewe and himself into a ram, seducing her in that shape. Their child was a golden sheep with the power of flight. The purpose of the legendary voyage of Jason and the Argonauts was to bring back the golden fleece of this beast to Greece.

Scylla and Charybdis: Terrors of the Sea

The channel between Italy and Sicily is dangerous for sailors, with unexpected whirlpools and currents. These natural phenomena inspired tales of Scylla and Charybdis, terrors of the Straits of Messina.

Once Poseidon had seen the loveliness of Scylla, one of the Nereids, he could think of nothing else. His desire for her was overwhelming and he pursued her openly. When Amphitrite, his wife, heard of this affair she was seized by jealousy. To punish her rival, she secretly poured the juice of some poisonous herbs into the waters of the fountain where Scylla often bathed.

As soon as the nymph stepped into the pool she was transformed into a monster with twelve feet and six heads, each one with a mouth containing three rows of teeth; the lower part of her body was turned into a pack of dogs who barked incessantly. Terrified and appalled by her new form, Scylla hurled herself from the cliffs at the southern tip of Italy, but even this did not end her suffering. The gods confined her in a cave looking out over the sea, where she was condemned to remain forever, snapping at any vessels that came near her.

Sailors were unable to avoid her ghastly attacks by steering a course farther out to sea, because there Charybdis—once a woman, now a vicious whirlpool—lay in wait. She was the daughter of Poseidon and Gaia, but despite this noble heritage, she was greedy, and had dared to try and steal Heracles' precious oxen. Outraged by her impertinence and avarice, Heracles complained to Zeus, his father, who struck her with a thunderbolt. She fell into the sea, just across from Scylla, and continued life as a whirlpool, which three times a day sucked down vast quantities of sea water and three times a day spewed it out again.

In the seas around Greece and Italy, seasonal storms and dangerous currents still bedevil sailors.

Many brave sailors perished when sea captains, trying to avoid Charybdis's greedy maw that pulled whole ships down into the depths, veered too close to the cliffs. There Scylla waited to snatch mariners from the decks. Or in a desperate attempt to avoid Scylla's jaws, a ship would drift into the spiraling arms of Charybdis. "Caught between Scylla and Charybdis" became a saying used to describe anyone trapped between two dangerous choices, where to avoid one peril means inevitably confronting another.

Hades, God of the Underworld

The third of the victorious sons of Cronus and Rhea was Hades. When their father's kingdom was divided, he was given the Underworld, not only the lands where the dead dwelt (see page 108) but also everything that lay beneath the surface of the Earth. So Hades was king of death, funerals, and the deceased, and of the agricultural riches and minerals of the Earth, and therefore of wealth itself. For this reason, he was known to the Romans as Pluto or Dis, both of which mean "wealth."

The Greeks and Romans were lovers of life and showed little interest in the rewards offered to the virtuous after death. For the Greeks in particular, the heroic ideal held that it was important to achieve glory during one's time on Earth. Occasionally a mortal beloved by the gods was given a form of immortality as a star, a constellation, or a plant, but for the most part death was unnervingly permanent and the afterlife could not be relied on to bring any reward for goodness in life. At the same time, the Greeks, and the Romans even more markedly, were deeply moralistic and believed that the wicked would be punished.

Perhaps because of this combination of concepts, Hades was seen as a dark and unattractive god, hard-hearted and merciless. He was generally unaware of what was happening among mortals or on Olympus—he remained instead in his realm under the Earth. His reluctance to ascend from the Underworld emphasized the permanence of death. He was also the supreme god of the chthonic or earth deities (see page 10), and was sometimes referred to as Chthonian Zeus.

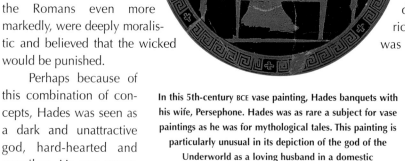

In this 5th-century BCE vase painting, Hades banquets with his wife, Persephone. Hades was as rare a subject for vase paintings as he was for mythological tales. This painting is particularly unusual in its depiction of the god of the Underworld as a loving husband in a domestic scene—mostly, he is shown on his throne.

Hades had the ability to remain unseen, because during the war against the Titans the Cyclopes gave him a helmet that rendered its wearer invisible, so that one could never see death approaching. When Hades *was* seen, he was often carrying keys—an indication that there was no way out of his kingdom.

His personal appearance was so grim and his residence was so dismal that he was unable to persuade any of the goddesses to marry him willingly, despite his power and his riches. Unlike his brothers he was seldom associated with seduction and consequently produced few if any offspring. His frustration at being unable to win a wife led him to abduct Persephone from her mother, Demeter, and to attempt to install her as queen of the Underworld (see pages 55–9) in what was one of the most dramatic episodes of classical myth.

Hades was surrounded by a strange court. The Erinyes—or Furies—were regarded by some of the poets as his daughters, and the three (or sometimes four) of them are often shown standing beside his throne (see page 107). They were of fearsome appearance, often garbed in black cloaks soaked in blood, wielding whips of scorpions, and with snakes instead of hair. They relentlessly enacted the vengeance of the gods, above all on those who murdered their own kin. When the Greeks dared to address them directly, they often called them the Eumenides, the benevolent ones. In myth, they were said to have earned this name by ending their persecution of a young man, Orestes, who killed his mother to avenge her murder of his father. However, it was also a superstition to refer to dark forces with flattering names, in order to ward off their evil power. Another companion of Hades was Hecate, a goddess associated with ghosts, black magic and crossroads (see page 79).

With the exception of his role in the tale of Persephone, Hades rarely features in classical mythology. In the stories of punishment after death, or of the living humans who visited his dark country, he is seldom involved personally. When he is, a softer, almost pitiful aspect to his character is shown. Even in the abduction of Persephone, Hades' loneliness makes him a sad figure. In the account of Orpheus's journey to the Underworld to reclaim his young wife (see page 109), Hades is said to have wept when he heard Orpheus's music and was so moved that he allowed Orpheus to try to take his wife back to the land of the living.

Nonetheless Hades does not have a fully rounded, almost human character like the other Olympian gods. This is partly a result of his chastity. With the exception of his abduction of Persephone, he did not become involved in the passions, intrigues, and jealousies that make up so much of the narrative of classical mythology. It is as if the classical authors felt uneasy telling stories about so dark a power.

Little religious ritual built up around Hades. Although he was acknowledged as part of the Olympian pantheon, no temples were built to him. Only black animals, usually black bulls, were sacrificed to him, and after the bull's throat was cut, the blood was not collected in vessels or sprinkled on an altar as it was at other sacrifices, but was left to drain down into the earth. Cypress trees, narcissi, and the maidenhair fern were all sacred to Hades, as was the number two, which was always regarded as inauspicious.

Hades greets a mythological hero as he arrives in the Underworld, on this ornate vase dating from *c.* 325 BCE and made in a Greek colony in Italy.

53

Demeter: A Tale of Rebirth

Demeter, the goddess of corn and harvest, of agriculture and country life, was a fertility goddess, a strong mother, always ready to nourish the Earth and make it fruitful. She was central to one of the most powerful classical myths explaining the cycle of the seasons.

Despite its commercial and cultural development over the centuries, the central and western Mediterranean remained throughout antiquity an agricultural region dependent on the annual success of crops and the fertility of all domesticated animals. Although foreign trade provided some essential goods as well as many luxuries, it was not sufficiently developed to supply the daily needs of a growing populace. Demeter, as the goddess of agricultural fertility, represented an essential life-force. She was probably based in the most ancient culture of the region and was often associated with the previous generations of the gods as much as with the Olympians. For the Greeks, she was sometimes identical to Rhea, or even Gaia, the Earth herself. Later, when the Greeks and Romans incorporated aspects of Egyptian legends into their own mythology, Demeter was also identified with Isis, who was, like her, a goddess of rebirth and fertility (see page 15).

Although she rarely appears in the adventures of the deities and heroes, Demeter was popular among both gods and humankind. She was always welcome on Olympus, but she preferred to stay on the Earth, where she wandered freely, looking after the cornfields. The island of Sicily and the countryside of Attica were regarded as her particular homes. She was typically represented wearing a crown made of ears of corn, holding a lighted torch or a cornucopia in one hand and a poppy in the other, but there were other, stranger images of her. In Sicily she was often shown heavily veiled in black and with the head of a horse: this depiction is probably connected with the story that Poseidon, the sea god, coupled with her when they had both disguised themselves as horses. Because of this same story, she is sometimes shown carrying a dolphin, the fish that was Poseidon's companion. In a more rural tradition she could be shown dressed as a country-

In this 2nd-century BCE Greek sculpture, Demeter holds a horn of plenty in one hand and a bouquet of corn and poppies in the other, both of which symbolize the fertility of nature.

Nature Spirits

The Greeks and Romans saw nature as full of divinity. They believed that some spirits inhabited rivers and forests and others personified natural forces. These beings were popular subjects for Greek and Roman art.

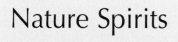

Nature spirits feature in the earliest surviving classical myths. And even in later, more sophisticated times, the Greeks and Romans felt a strong connection to the natural world.

Many of these spirits belonged to a specific place. For example, almost all rivers, springs, and fountains had their own individual guardian spirits or gods. Other figures were more generic. The Nereids, children of Pontus and Gaia, and the Oceanids, children of two Titans, were sea nymphs; the Dryads and Hamadryads presided over woodlands; while the Oreads were responsible for hills and mountains. There were also minor nature gods with more specific duties. Triton, for

This sleeping woodland spirit was carved in Greece in the 3rd century BCE.

example, was responsible for calming storms; Priapus was the god of gardens and reproductive organs; and Aurora was goddess of the dawn.

The chief of these diverse spirits was Pan, god of the countryside and of goatherds and shepherds. He lived in wild places accompanied by satyrs, male nature spirits who were half-man and half-goat. With his horns and hairy goat's legs, he was so ugly that no nymph would have him as a mate, but he made beautiful music on his pipes.

woman, riding on an ox, with a basket on her left arm, and a hoe in her right hand. In a less rustic context she was seen driving a chariot pulled by a pair of dragons.

In the spring, a pregnant pig was sacrificed to her, no doubt partly because pigs were regarded as highly fertile owing to the size of their litters, and partly because pregnant sows are notorious for the damage they can do to new crops. In Sicily she was also offered a ram that was led three times around a field before having its throat cut in ritual fashion.

Demeter features in one of the most important classical myths, which explains the annual cycle of the seasons, the rhythms of sowing and

harvesting, the contrast between summer and winter. Although the emphasis might change in accordance with local tradition, this tale of Demeter and Persephone remained unusually consistent throughout the classical period.

Zeus remained close to Demeter, his sister, even after his marriage to Hera, and was, indeed, the father of her daughter, Persephone. Although Hera was ordinarily deeply jealous of Zeus's relationships with other women, there are no stories of her feeling resentment toward Demeter. This is because it was acceptable for Olympian gods to be involved in incestuous unions.

Demeter was a more careful and devoted mother than any of the other goddesses, and she doted on her daughter, the beautiful Persephone. Demeter arranged for her to be brought up in Sicily and educated and accompanied by a troupe of nymphs (young female nature spirits).

Hades, god of the Underworld, was attracted to Persephone and with the tacit approval of Zeus, her father and his brother, he decided to abduct her. In one version of this story, Aphrodite, the goddess of love, deliberately caused Hades to fall in love with Persephone, because she was reluctant to see too many attractive young women choose to remain chaste. Hades found Persephone gathering flowers near the slopes of Mount Etna. Ignoring her cries, he swept her up into his chariot and carried her away. On the shores of Lake Cyane in Sicily he struck the ground and it opened up for him so that he could carry his victim down into his kingdom.

Demeter searched for Persephone throughout Sicily, by day and even by night using torches lit from the volcano of Mount Etna, but without success. Thereafter she wandered, half mad, across the world looking for her child, or at least for news of her. During these searches she refused to perform any of her duties, and as a result crops failed, farm animals became infertile, and the world suffered from desperate famine.

After wandering for months, Demeter gave in to despair, and she sat on a rock in Attica for nine days, weeping. This rock was traditionally the foundation stone of Eleusis, which became the site of Demeter's greatest sanctuary (see page 58).

A procession of worshippers brings sacrifices to Demeter in a Greek marble sculpture dating from the end of the 4th century BCE. The person at the front of the procession is offering her a spring lamb.

She was rescued from her misery by the kindness of Celeus, king of Attica, and his wife Metaneira, who took her home and comforted her, even though they believed she was just a mad old woman. In gratitude she cured Demophon, their infant son, who was dying of a fever. She wanted to make him immortal and began to perform a magic ritual, which included laying the boy in the fire to burn away his mortality, but she was interrupted by his mother, who was terrified by the sight of her son in the fire. Although Demophon therefore remained mortal, Demeter blessed him. She also blessed Celeus's and Metaneira's other son, Triptolemus, and when he was old enough she instructed him in the art of agriculture, so that he was able to pass on the skills to humanity.

After this interlude Demeter returned to her search. Accounts vary as to who finally told her the truth about her daughter's disappearance: some versions say that it was Arethusa, a river nymph; another that it was Hecate, the goddess of ghosts and witches; and some that it was a shepherd who heard the tale from another who had witnessed Persephone's abduction first-hand. As soon as she received this crucial information, Demeter rushed to Olympus to demand that Zeus exercise his powers and restore their daughter to her. Zeus tried to persuade her that Hades, an Olympian and a powerful god, was a suitable husband for Persephone, but Demeter remained resolute in her desire to have her daughter back. Her mourning, and therefore the famine, continued.

Flowers in Myth

Springtime in the Mediterranean comes suddenly and is marked by a profusion of wild flowers in woodlands and fields. This almost magical transformation of the landscape moved the classical storytellers deeply. Flowers occur frequently in cult, in myth, and in poetry and have a range of symbolic meanings.

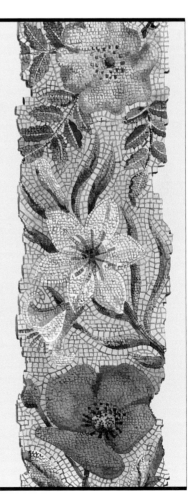

Flowers, meadow flowers in particular, were a symbol of innocence and purity as well as beauty. The Graces (see page 63) were usually illustrated adorned with flowers, and the gathering and garlanding of flowers was one of the principal activities of nymphs and woodland spirits. Flowers were the particular symbols of young girls and virgins: Persephone was gathering them when she was abducted by Hades; and Europa (see page 47) was collecting wild flowers with her friends when she encountered Zeus as a bull.

Because of their medicinal and hallucinogenic uses, flowers were also extremely powerful and thus were worthy of association with the Olympians. Each of the goddesses had particular flowers associated with her: the rose was sacred to Aphrodite; the poppy to Demeter, since it blossoms in cornfields; and the lily to Hera, whose milk was said to have dyed the flower white. The gods also transformed human beings they were particularly fond of, such as Adonis (see pages 126–8), into flowers after death in order to immortalize their memories.

The Eleusinian Mysteries

Every year, for more than 2,000 years, the Greeks celebrated a strange and solemn festival in thanks for Demeter's gift of agriculture to humanity. The Eleusinian Mysteries, as they were known, were so highly regarded that some people esteemed them above even the Olympic Games.

The cult, with its main sanctuary at Eleusis, only 15 miles (24 km) from Athens, was essentially egalitarian. Men and women of all ages could be initiated on equal terms, and the celebrations were designed so that there was no distinction between rich and poor. To ensure this, anyone arriving in Eleusis in a chariot was very heavily fined. The only people barred from admission were serious criminals, practitioners of witchcraft, and anyone who had, even accidentally, taken another's life.

Initiation into the Mysteries earned a person a special relationship with all the gods, securing happiness and success, and guaranteeing privileges in the Underworld. Members of the cult were bound to secrecy, and to reveal the rituals was to risk severe punishment, even death. Because of this, scholars know little about what happened during the ceremonies. What is known, thanks to comments by several writers including Pindar and Sophocles, is that the participants in the rites at Eleusis found the festival emotionally satisfying.

A year before attending the great Mysteries, candidates had to go through a lesser ritual that began with an extensive purification rite. The actual moment of initiation was terrifying: hallucinatory visions and specters appeared, the temple shook, hideous noises sounded, lightning flashed, and there was a background of either intense dark or leaping flames. After initiation the new cult members could join a nine-day festival, the Greater Mysteries, which included processions, ritual baths, games, sacrifices, libations, and chanting.

A scene from an initiation into the Eleusinian Mysteries, showing a priest with an initiate, is depicted in this Roman mosaic, dating from the 1st century CE, and found in Valpolicella. Because initiates were sworn to secrecy, little is known about the rites. Roman mosaics and wall paintings therefore offer valuable insights into these esoteric religious practices.

Finally Zeus relented. He agreed that Hades should be made to give up his bride provided that she had not eaten anything in the Underworld: it was impossible to return to Earth after eating the food of the dead. Unfortunately Persephone had swallowed seven pomegranate seeds. Even Hades did not know this, but she was betrayed by Ascalaphus, one of Hades's gardeners. Demeter turned him into an owl in her anger, which is why the bird is a symbol of ill omen.

Eventually a compromise was reached. Persephone would remain the bride of Hades and would live with him for six months of the year, but for the other six months she was allowed to return to her mother. When Persephone was on the Earth, Demeter was happy and made the world fruitful, but during the time her daughter spent with Hades, Demeter mourned and nothing grew.

This myth appealed to the Greeks and Romans on many levels. Not only is it a touching story of the love between a mother and daughter, but it also explores the natural cycle of seasonal death and rebirth. In doing so, it addresses one of humankind's essential fears—that the Earth might cease to be fertile and the barren winter months never end. The involvement of the Olympian gods, and Demeter's desire to see her daughter again after a long, lonely winter, made it inevitable, in very human terms, that spring would reappear each year.

The worship of Demeter was widespread. Most cities and islands told tales of her visit to them during her long search for her daughter, but of all these places Sicily and Eleusis were the two most sacred to her. In Sicily there was a huge, annual festival in her honor, during which bulls were sacrificed by Lake Cyane. The celebration at Eleusis was the most important religious event in Greece. In Rome, where Demeter was known as Ceres, there was an annual festival in her honor in April during which married women would give up drink and intercourse for a week—thus abstaining from both reproductive acts and physical pleasure—and would parade through the streets at night carrying torches.

In this delicate 5th-century BCE Greek vase painting, a woman brings an offering to an altar. Like the other Greek gods, Demeter was propitiated with offerings and sacrifices, typically of pigs and sheep. In Rome, where she was known as Ceres, her worship was particularly important to women.

THE RENAISSANCE AND THE GODS

For almost a millennium after the classical world came to an end, the Christian Church tried to suppress representations of the Olympian gods in art. That situation changed in fifteenth-century Italy when a generation of humanist scholars, in reaction against what they regarded as the superstition of the preceding age, turned to classical culture as an ideal of rational enlightenment. Painters and sculptors followed suit, taking Greek and Roman mythology as favored subjects for their works. Ironically, one of their greatest patrons was the Papacy, which had for so long denounced the gods as pagan figures.

Above: This detail from Botticelli's famous *Birth of Venus* shows the goddess arriving on the shore of Cyprus, fully grown. According to myth, Venus was conceived when the sperm from her castrated father, Uranus, mixed with the waves to generate a foam from which she was born.

Right: Renaissance artists were fascinated by Diana, whose passion for the hunt challenged the sexual stereotypes of the time. This portrait, *Diana the Huntress*, showing the goddess blowing her horn, was painted by Orazio Gentileschi.

Left: *The Origin of the Milky Way* by Tintoretto shows Heracles suckling at the breast of Hera—when he pulled away, a splash of milk created the belt of stars.

Below: Caravaggio's portrait of the young Bacchus presents the god in the guise of a decadent Roman.

Above: Designed by Raphael and executed by his pupils, this ceiling from the Villa Farnesina in Rome shows the gods assembled in council to discuss the fate of Cupid and his human lover, Psyche. Zeus is seated on his throne, right.

Aphrodite, Goddess of Love

Aphrodite, the goddess of love, marriage, and beauty, personified not only romantic love but also sexual passion, and her unearthly charm attracted both gods and mortals. Throughout the centuries artists rivaled one another in their attempts to capture her beauty, helping to make her perhaps the best known of the classical gods.

There are two main mythic traditions associated with the origins of Aphrodite, which are reflected in the epithets that were commonly attached to her name. Some accounts describe her as the daughter of Zeus and a nymph, Dione: as the fruit of Zeus's philandering, she was the personification of attraction and physical love. This was Aphrodite Pandemos, or Aphrodite of the people.

Another version of Aphrodite's birth makes her the most senior and venerable of all the Olympian deities. This portrays her as Aphrodite Urania, the offspring of Uranus, the first sky god, and therefore a survivor from the earliest times (see

The newborn Aphrodite is lifted from the sea by two of the Graces, her handmaidens. Dating from the 5th century BCE, this carving once adorned the back of a chair.

page 27). In this tradition, she represents sacred love. When Cronus castrated his father, Uranus, he flung his parts into the ocean. There his semen mixed with the sea foam, and from that union, untainted by sexual contact, Aphrodite was conceived. The tides and winds of the sea carried her gently first to the island of Cythera and then to Cyprus where she was brought up by the Graces. When the Olympians defeated Cronus, she was taken to Olympus, where the gods, moved by her beauty, welcomed her.

Aphrodite therefore represented both sacred and profane love. She was goddess of harlotry and prostitution, but also of marriage. She led women into adultery, but also encouraged them to be faithful and chaste. She punished viciously, but rewarded generously. These mixed messages are consistent with the conflicting versions of her beginnings. She existed before the Olympians came into being, but she was younger and lovelier than any of the other goddesses. She was patroness of physical love and therefore of procreation and the future of civilization, but at the same time she delighted in bawdy comedy.

The different ways in which Aphrodite has been represented in art illustrate the two sides to her nature. Sometimes she is depicted as a fertility goddess, with exaggerated physical attributes. More often, however, she is portrayed as an idealized version of femininity, as typified by the renowned Venus de Milo (see page 122). In these images she is often depicted wearing her famous girdle. Any woman who wore this magical belt became instantly beautiful and desirable to the eyes of whoever saw her. Even Hera, who seldom associated with Aphrodite, was known to have borrowed the girdle to rekindle Zeus's desire for her. It was so powerful that when Aphrodite herself wore it, even her infuriated and cuckolded husband, Hephaestus, was happy to forgive her all her infidelities.

This ambiguity inherent in Aphrodite's imagery is shown in a story about the Greek sculptor Praxiteles, who worked in the second half of the third century BCE and was noted for his carvings in Parian marble, the shining white stone

A detail from a 1st-century CE fresco in Pompeii shows two of the Three Graces, companions of Aphrodite. As the goddess of beauty, she drew to her the most attractive of the divine beings.

particularly prized by Greek sculptors. Praxiteles was invited to make a statue of Aphrodite for a temple on the island of Cos. He was not sure which image of the goddess the purchasers wanted, so he made two, one presenting the sensual side of Aphrodite and the other showing her veiled. The people of Cos preferred the latter statue, even though the naked Aphrodite was superior in workmanship, because the priests wished to encourage modesty and decorum—since it was the fashion for the women of Cos to wear white garments of cloth so fine that it was transparent, perhaps this ambition was wise. The people of Cnidos, however, bought the naked statue for their temple. It was said to be so beautiful that one young man broke into the temple at night to try to gratify his desire for the goddess.

All the male gods were fascinated by Aphrodite's beauty. This made her unpopular with the other goddesses, especially with Hera, whose annoyance increased when Zeus attempted to seduce Aphrodite, despite the fact that she refused to submit to him even when he threatened her with violence. Because she was the goddess of passion, she had absolute control over lust and even Zeus was not able to rape her; instead, to punish her for her refusal, he forced her to marry Hephaestus, the least attractive of the Olympian gods.

Her marriage did not prevent Aphrodite from indulging in a long stream of relationships with both gods and mortals, and she had several children whose myths explore the kinds of love that came to humankind—mutual tenderness, mad passion, the love between humans and gods, and desire between men and women and men and men. Aphrodite had two children with

63

Hermes (see page 103), the messenger of the gods. The most famous of them was Eros, also known to the Romans as Cupid (see page 67), the winged god of passion, whose arrows caused his victims to fall in love instantly and totally, making them desperate with often unreciprocated desire. He frequently accompanied Aphrodite in her adventures or ran errands for her, typically causing those who had offended her to fall in love with inappropriate or unsympathetic people. Her second child by Hermes was Hermaphroditus, who fused with a sea nymph—their bodies were joined into one being, half-man and half-woman. With Dionysus, Aphrodite conceived Priapus, a fertility god.

Her most famous lover was Ares, the god of war. Their lengthy relationship scandalized even the free-living Olympians. With Ares, Aphrodite had two children. Anteros was the god of orderly, lawful love, and especially of shared tenderness. Although few stories were told about him, he was often depicted in paintings and vase decoration, usually wrestling with Eros. In Greek schools there was sometimes a wall painting of Anteros to remind students that it was their duty to love and respect their teachers.

Harmony was Aphrodite's second child by Ares. Her gentle nature demonstrated the way in which love can moderate the anger of conflict. She was given in marriage to Cadmus, the founder of Thebes. All the Olympian gods attended this wedding and showered the couple with gifts, including a famous necklace made for her by Hephaestus. But because Harmony was Aphrodite's child, she had unwittingly attracted the hatred of Hera, worse still, Cadmus was the brother of Europa (see page 47), another of Zeus's conquests, whom the divine consort disliked even more. So although the couple was virtuous, Hera ensured that nothing but tragedy befell the family.

Aphrodite was one of the most widely worshipped of all the Olympian goddesses because it was understood that without love there would be no life or future for humanity. As well as being the goddess of love, she was regarded as the patroness of beauty, elegance, pleasure, the graces, and social amenities. She was also the goddess of laughter, so comedy came under her influence. Roses, myrtles, and apples were sacred to Aphrodite, as were doves, swans and sparrows, and these birds

The Aphrodite of Cnidos, carved in Parian marble by the renowned sculptor Praxiteles in 340 BCE. It was offered first to the people of Cos, who were concerned it would discourage modesty.

shared the honor of drawing her chariot. In her temples, ritual prostitution or sex with fellow worshippers was sometimes practiced in addition to the offering of blood sacrifices, and there were frequent complaints about the excesses that occurred at some of her rites.

Aphrodite played a key role in the Trojan War, recorded in the great epics of Homer and Virgil. According to myth, the conflict started because the gods found a golden apple that was said to belong to the most beautiful goddess of all.

Aphrodite, Hera, and Athena all claimed their right to the prize and, too nervous to make a decision himself, Zeus appointed Paris, prince of Troy, to judge among them. Each of the three bribed Paris with some kind of honor, and Paris chose Aphrodite after she offered him the most beautiful woman in the world as his bride. Her rash promise led to the abduction of Helen, the wife of Menelaus, who was noted as the loveliest of mortals. Menelaus led an army of Greeks to Troy to reclaim her, initiating the ten-year war. Paris, in

Eos and Tithonus

Although far from faithful herself, Aphrodite was vindictive toward her rivals. Following the usual practice of Olympian goddesses, it was the woman, rather than the man, whom she blamed, and her punishments were always ferocious.

Although he enjoyed being with Aphrodite, Ares continued to seek his satisfaction wherever he desired, and he embarked on an affair with Eos, the goddess of the dawn.

One day Aphrodite caught the two together, and her jealousy was aroused. She pronounced a terrible curse on Eos. Never would she love a god again—she would desire only mortal men. And so it happened that Eos, a goddess, fell in love with Tithonus, a handsome prince of Troy. They were so happy together that he begged her to grant him the gift of everlasting life, and she foolishly agreed.

At first all seemed well. But they had forgotten to arrange for him to remain youthful and in good health. He grew older, more frail and decrepit, until his life became unbearable and he begged Eos to let him die peacefully.

She sought the help of Zeus, but even he could not take away the gift of another god. In the end, since Tithonus could neither live nor die, he was changed into a grasshopper, which ever since has greeted its former lover by chirping at the first light of dawn.

Aphrodite, a vengeful goddess when betrayed, is shown with her lover, Ares, in this 5th-century BCE votive relief.

Aphrodite rests in a giant shell, attended by Cupid, in this 1st-century Roman wall painting from Pompeii.

choosing Aphrodite, allied her with the Trojan side against the Greeks, who were favored by Hera and Athena.

Meanwhile Aphrodite had taken a human lover, Anchises, a Trojan nobleman, by whom she had a son, Aeneas. When the Greeks finally won the war and set the city of Troy on fire, Aphrodite intervened to assist her mortal child to escape, carrying his now aged father on his back. Although she was unable to protect him from the wrath of the other Olympians, she helped and guided him throughout ten years of travel and exile, as recorded in Virgil's *Aeneid*.

The Romans regarded Aeneas as the father of Rome because he founded the royal line that was later to build the city on the seven hills. In their desire to be perceived as a noble nation associated with the heroic stories of Greece and the eastern Mediterranean, the Romans found that Aeneas's parentage, with Aphrodite as his mother, provided them with the legitimacy they sought. Later the emperors claimed to be descended, through Aeneas, directly from the Olympian gods. Under the Romans, Aphrodite, then known as Venus, became a gentle, more dignified goddess of beauty and love, the queen of laughter and patron of social life and sensual pleasures, all of which the Romans enjoyed so much.

Cupid's Arrow

Eros, the quintessence of love, was originally a mysterious, primeval force. But with time he was gradually transformed into the familiar, winged figure of Cupid—the mischievous, cherubic infant equipped with the bow and arrows of desire.

As with Aphrodite, there are two traditions explaining Eros's or Cupid's birth. One associates him with the pre-Olympian world. The poet Hesiod told how Eros came into existence as the power of love at the very beginning of the world, along with Gaia (the Earth) and Tartarus (the Underworld). Other accounts say that the world came into being with the mating of Eros and Chaos, so that even the gods owe their existence to him.

Gradually, however, as the various myths and mythic themes consolidated around the individual gods, Aphrodite became the divine personification of love. But because his worship was so well established, Eros was assimilated into this new tradition as the son of Aphrodite. As the offspring of the goddess, Eros came to represent the masculine ideal of love, in the same way that Aphrodite represented the feminine ideal, and he was always depicted as being as young and beautiful as she was.

As the mythic tradition developed over the centuries and Zeus became more powerful, so, increasingly, Aphrodite was seen as his daughter, and therefore under his power like the other Olympians, rather than as a goddess born to Uranus, who

A 4th-century CE Roman mosaic shows several Cupids fishing. In this typical late depiction of the god, he is chubby and playful. The Romans often used images of Cupid as a decorative element in mosaics, frescoes, and carvings.

belonged to an earlier divine generation. Her loss of status affected her son. His appearance became less impressive: his wings and arrows were introduced, as were tales of his mischievous nature and his light-heartedness about passion.

When the Romans established their control over the body of myth, Cupid, as they called Eros, became less mysterious still. He was depicted both in stories and in art as a chubby child, often naughty, but always charming. He appeared in art as decoration, portrayed as a whimsical cherub, frequently playing with a hoop or a butterfly—in contrast to the mighty god he had originally been among the Greeks.

THE SECOND GENERATION

Zeus was not a solitary, distant god, who wanted only to be worshipped from afar. He and the entire household of Olympian gods were lovers of life. Classical myth is a testament to their passion and joyful exuberance as they ate, fought, and loved with gusto.

This divine energy was also expressed in the fecundity of many of the gods. A number of the lesser deities were the offspring of one of the Olympians and all the great heroes had at least one divine parent. Of the male Olympians, Zeus and Poseidon were especially voracious lovers, and Zeus in particular was the father of an enormous number of children, both mortals and gods. When he seduced or raped a woman or a nymph, she inevitably became pregnant.

Some of Zeus's children became recognized as Olympians themselves. It is not clear why certain of them achieved that honor while others of equally prestigious parentage did not, but it is likely that it had much to do with the ways in which the separate areas of Greece and the eastern Mediterranean came together gradually to form a unified culture, each bringing its own local deities to the mix. The status of a new god was determined by how important or influential his or her territory was. Mythographers have pointed out that the origins of the six gods of the second generation of Olympians are geographically very diverse: Dionysus came from the East; Artemis originated on the Turkish mainland and the Greek islands; Athena was a major deity of both Egypt and Greece; and Ares' power was greatest in the western Italian peninsula.

The make-up of the Olympian family itself was fluid. In the earliest tradition there were fourteen Olympian gods, a number later reduced to the twelve that is familiar today. Hestia, the goddess of the hearth (see page 105) and a daughter of Cronus and Rhea, once was counted among the Olympians but was later replaced by Dionysus (see pages 91–5). Hades is sometimes replaced by Hermes, a son of Zeus (see pages 100–103).

The characters of the second generation of Olympians are the most complex and developed. Stemming from later traditions than their elders, they reflect the broad spectrum of Greek and Roman personalities.

Above: Poseidon, Aphrodite, Apollo and Athena are shown with Pan on this Greek vase from 340 BCE.

Opposite: A relief carving from *c.* 400 BCE showing Zeus, seated, with his two children Apollo (*center*) and Artemis (*right*), and an unknown deity.

69

Athena, Goddess of Good Counsel

Of all his children, Zeus was fondest of his daughter Athena, the virgin goddess of wisdom, who presided over crafts and skills, including those associated with both war and peace. She was the patron of Athens, and her prestige increased with the city's fortunes, so that as it became the preeminent Greek city her status among the Olympians grew.

The story of the birth of Athena, who was to become Zeus's closest and best-loved companion, contains the same elements as other myths about the birth of gods. Just as Uranus and Cronus feared (rightly so) that their children would supplant them, Zeus knew he also might be supplanted by one of his offspring.

In the older accounts of the story, typified by Hesiod's *Theogony*, Metis, the Titan goddess of prudence and sagacity, became pregnant by Zeus. Fearful that the child might prove to be more wise and powerful than he was, and encouraged by Gaia and Uranus, Zeus swallowed Metis, hoping to kill the unborn child but at the same time keeping the Titaness's wisdom for himself. Some months later he developed an agonizing headache. Such was the pain that he commanded Hephaestus to cut his head open with an axe. Athena sprang, adult and fully armed, from the gash.

In many myths Athena opposes or counterpoints Aphrodite: reason against passion, wisdom against beauty. As patron of Athens, the first city of Greece, Athena came to stand for everything Greek culture most valued. In many of the stories about her, she represents the power of intelligence and self-possession, of knowledge and sagacity. She is committed to chastity and remains unswayed by the irrationality of love or passion.

The moment of Athena's birth is depicted on this Athenian cup dating from *c.* 550 BCE. Hephaestus, the divine smith, has split Zeus's head with an axe, and Athena emerges from the wound, fully grown and armed with a shield. Because of this unique birth, father and daughter always shared a special bond.

The Contest over Athens

Athena was the patron goddess of Athens, and her great temple, the Parthenon, dominated the city from its high rock (see pages 74–5). She had won the accolade as a prize in recognition of her wisdom and her generosity to humankind.

Cecrops, king of Attica in Greece, encouraged the tribes of the region to join together to create a city-state. The gods watched Cecrops from Olympus, and knew that the city he was building would become one of the greatest in the world. Not surprisingly, many of the gods wanted to be its patron, leading to heated debate about who deserved this privilege. Eventually, it was recognized that two deities had the best claims: Poseidon, because the city was close to the sea, his domain; and Athena because the arts of civilized life were bound to flourish there.

Neither would give way to the other, and even Zeus was alarmed at the consequences of a quarrel between two such powerful Olympians. So he proposed a competition, to be judged by the other gods. Each contestant was challenged to produce a novelty for humanity, something both useful and beautiful, and whoever came up with the finest invention would be given the new city as a prize.

Poseidon immediately struck the ground with his trident and a huge black animal appeared, tossing its mane and pawing the ground. It was strong, fast and beautiful, yet amenable—the first horse. The gods, impressed, imagined that the matter was settled, but Athena, smiling gently, instantly produced out of the rocky soil a tree with grey leaves and small oval green fruits—the olive.

The olive, she pointed out, would provide both food for human beings and oil for sacrifices to the gods. The tree would be hardy and enduring, bearing fruit even in the roughest, driest ground. But what is more important, she said, is that the olive tree represents peace, while the horse represents war. Surely peace was more useful to mortals and more beautiful than war?

Although none of the gods wanted to offend Poseidon and they all admired his magnificent invention, they were forced to acknowledge that Athena was the winner. Her olive tree was one of the most precious gifts the gods ever gave the people of Greece. Amid the cheers of the Olympians, the nascent city received a name and a powerful patron at the same time.

The olive tree, a gift from Athena to the people of Greece, has remained a staple of Greek agriculture.

Nonetheless, she did have a child. Hephaestus wanted to marry her, and when she refused he attempted to rape her. She resisted him successfully, but afterward she had to wipe his seed off her body with a tuft of wool that she then threw down on to the Earth. From this botched coupling, Erichthonius, a strange monster with a man's body but a serpent's tail instead of legs, was born.

Despite the circumstances of his conception, and the fact that she had never carried him in her womb, Athena took responsibility for him, arranged his upbringing and education, and eventually made him king of Athens. After he died she transformed him into a star in the constellation Auriga, the charioteer.

Apart from this episode, there are no stories about Athena having romantic involvements. Instead she became known as a protector of heroes: Jason who led the Argonauts in search of the Golden Fleece; Orestes, who murdered his adulterous mother, Clytemnestra; Theseus, who slew the Minotaur and became king of Athens; Heracles (Hercules to the Romans); and Odysseus, whose ten-year journey back to his home after the Trojan War was recounted in Homer's *Odyssey*.

Among her favorites was Perseus, a son of Zeus by one of his mistresses, and therefore a victim of Hera's jealousy Athena protected and advised him through his adventures. To help him slay Medusa, the monstrous Gorgon with hair of writhing snakes, she lent him her magical shield. Perseus used this as a mirror to approach the Gorgon obliquely since any direct glance into her hideous face immediately turned a man to stone. After Perseus came back triumphant from this adventure, he returned the shield to Athena, and also gave her Medusa's head. In art, the image of this head is emblazoned in the center of Athena's shield or on her breastplate or helmet.

Athena was involved in both the public and the personal lives of almost every member of society. As the goddess of useful skills and crafts, she watched over military competence, but unlike Poseidon and Ares she was never seen as a bloodthirsty warrior. She was equally interested

This sculpture of Athena, carved between 525 and 520 BCE, adorned one of the temples on the Acropolis (see pages 74–5), the main religious complex of Athens, set on a hill overlooking the city. It was there that the citizens of Athens constructed the Parthenon, the magnificent temple dedicated to Athena, in the 5th century BCE.

in the creative arts of spinning and weaving, and is sometimes shown seated in full armor, but with a distaff for spinning wool or flax in her right hand instead of a spear. Athenians looked to her as patron of their children's education and of the building of houses and temples. She also had a special relationship with sailors since she was believed to have invented the first ship and taught humanity how to sail it. Above all, she alone among the gods could assuage the anger of Zeus, and even persuade him to change his mind.

Like the other Olympians Athena could be jealous or spiteful. For example, she gave her unqualified support to the Greeks throughout the Trojan War, because Paris, the prince of Troy, had judged her less beautiful than Aphrodite, even though she had offered him immortal fame as a hero to award the prize to her. Equally severe was her treatment of Arachne, a presumptuous young woman who was a noted weaver and embroiderer. Despite warnings, she challenged Athena to a contest of skill, which Athena accepted. In the Roman poet Ovid's retelling of this story, Athena wove a picture showing the triumphs of the gods while Arachne created a series of pictures showing their vices, particularly the lusts of Zeus. Athena not only won the competition, but she also punished her competitor for daring to issue the challenge by turning her into a spider.

The worship of Athena, particularly in Athens, took place in impressive settings and involved intricate rituals. Her temple, the Parthenon, dominated the city. One of the rituals in her worship involved young boys, wearing full armor, performing a dance in imitation of the great victory ritual that Athena was said to have staged for the Olympian gods to celebrate the defeat of the Titans.

The Names of Athena

Like all the other Olympian divinities, Athena had a number of different names, or epithets. Some of these were regional variations, others referred to part of her function or her nature, and others again described aspects of her worship.

Athena, armed with a shield and a spear, on the reverse of a silver tetradrachma, a Greek coin, dating from c. 324 BCE.

Athena is most frequently known as Pallas Athena. The name derives from an episode during the war against the Titans (see pages 32–5) when she personally fought and killed Pallas, a son of Uranus and Gaia. Following her victory she dressed herself in his skin and so took on his powers, his masculine strength adding to her womanly wisdom.

She was also called "Parthenos," from the Greek word for a virgin, in honor of her unwavering chastity; "Glaukopis," after her clear, bluish-grey eyes; "Hippia," "horsewoman," because she taught mortals how to tame horses; "Coryphagenes," or "born from the head," to describe her birth from Zeus's head; and "Athena Sais," because she was worshipped particularly in that Egyptian city. Each of these names was associated with a specific emblem. As Pallas Athena she was accompanied by an owl, the symbol of wisdom, whereas the imagery of Sais crowned her helmet with a cockerel. And as Athena Parthenos she sat on a throne, fully armed with shield and spear.

THE CITY ON THE HILL

To the millions of tourists who visit it each year, the Acropolis (literally, "high city") in the Greek capital of Athens is an architectural showplace. But for the ancient Greeks, the site had a more profound significance. Part walled citadel and part civic center, the 984-foot-long (300-m) complex was also a sacred precinct dedicated to the Olympian gods. Pride of place went to the city's patron, Athena. A 39-foot-high (12-m) sculpture of the goddess stood in her great temple, the Parthenon, and all twelve Olympian deities were celebrated on the building's eastern frieze. A much-used theater on the southern slope of the hill was dedicated to Dionysus.

Above: Built in the 5th century BCE, Athena's magnificent temple, the Parthenon, was the Acropolis's ceremonial centerpiece. Sculptures on the building depicted scenes from her life and the nature of her worship.

Above: Despite the ravages of time, the Acropolis dominates the Athenian skyline today just as it did in classical times. Many of the gods had sanctuaries on the sacred hilltop.

Right: The Theater of Herodes Atticus was built on the Acropolis in the 2nd century CE. Similar theaters were built throughout the Greek world. Ancient Greek plays are still staged in the amphitheater today.

Left: Statues dating from the late 5th century BCE support the roof of the Porch of the Caryatids in the Erechtheion. This temple contained altars to Athena, Poseidon and Hephaestus.

Below: This section from the sculpted frieze that once decorated the Parthenon shows horses carrying their riders bareback as part of the great procession that introduced the annual Panathenaea, the festival in Athena's honor.

Artemis, Virgin Huntress

Artemis was the virgin goddess of the hunt, of uncultivated land and wild animals, as well as of the moon. She preferred the wilderness and the woodlands to cities, had few dealings with men, and seldom visited Olympus.

Artemis was born from Zeus's passion for Leto, daughter of two Titans and famous for her beauty. Hera discovered his infidelity and persecuted Leto with an ingenious range of cruelties. First she sent a terrible serpent, the Python, to torture the pregnant woman. To protect Leto and her unborn child, Zeus turned her into a quail so that she could fly away, but even this did not end his wife's persecution of the lovely young woman. Hera, unrelenting, refused to allow Leto to return to the ground to give birth.

As Leto flew desperately out over the sea, the island of Delos took pity on her and allowed her access on condition that it would be established as the cult center of the god to whom she was about to give birth. Once she was safe on the island, Zeus transformed her into a woman again and she went into labor leaning against a palm tree.

First she gave birth to Artemis, but her labor continued. The newly born goddess had to watch her mother's struggles, and assisted her to give birth to her twin brother, Apollo. So shocked was Artemis by this experience of childbirth that she told her father, Zeus, that she wanted to be allowed to remain a virgin always, and also to be given the power to assist all women in childbirth. She shared her role as protector of childbirth with Hera herself and with Eileithyia, who was a daughter of Zeus and Hera but not one of the Olympian gods.

Artemis's most important role was as the goddess of women and of female secrets. She was also closely associated with the moon, whose four-week cycle of waxing and waning relates to the female 28-day fertility cycle. As the protectress of women, she had special concern for adolescent girls, for women in labor and for women who wished to remain virgins.

Preferring the company of women and shunning the presence of men as far as possible, Artemis lived as a huntress, roaming the wildest parts of the countryside. She was served by sixty of the Oceanids, and accompanied by other nymphs and mortals who were all virgins. Artemis was also associated with the Amazons, a tribe of wild women warriors who lived in the eastern hinterland of what is now Turkey. They mated with men only once a year and they

Because of her role as a fertility goddess, Artemis was sometimes depicted as having many breasts, as in this marble statue of the 2nd century CE from Ephesus, in modern-day Turkey.

Right: Diana, the Roman equivalent to Artemis, was most commonly associated with hunting, as in this 1st-century CE Roman fresco from Stabia, near Naples, Italy. The town was destroyed in the eruption of Mount Vesuvius in 79 CE.

The Islands of Greece

The eastern Mediterranean is scattered with islands: besides the major Aegean archipelagoes of the Cyclades and the Dodecanese, many small islands fringe mainland Greece and Asia Minor. Several religious cults and myths have their origins here.

The gods were often said to have been born or brought up on islands. For example, Artemis and Apollo started life on Delos, near Mykonos in the middle of the Cyclades. Aphrodite came ashore and grew up on Cythera or, in some versions, Cyprus. When Hephaestus was thrown down from Olympus, he landed on Lemnos where he set up his forges, and where he always worked. Zeus was secretly brought up in Crete; and Hera, when she could no longer tolerate living with Zeus, found refuge on Euboea. Demeter's favored home was the island of Sicily, and it was from here that her daughter was abducted; in her mad, wandering search for Persephone, she visited most of the islands of the Aegean, as did Dionysus in his journey from the east.

Every island seems to have contributed a god, a myth or an immortal. The genius of the Greek imagination lay in synthesizing these tales into manageable, interconnected narratives. Common themes found throughout them, such as the constant travels of the gods, allowed storytellers to incorporate different island traditions into one coherent body of myth. The atmosphere of multiplicity and variety, and the notion of metamorphosis (magical change and fluidity), were also creative responses to the challenge presented by the unique geography of the Mediterranean region.

There are hundreds of islands in the Mediterranean, and many were sacred to the gods.

immediately destroyed any male children who were born to them.

Although fiercely protective of these women, Artemis dealt ruthlessly with those who broke their vows of chastity. One of her attendants was a lovely young princess named Callisto, who was seduced by Zeus disguised as Artemis herself. Later, when Callisto was bathing with Artemis, the goddess noticed that she was pregnant. Furious, she refused to accept even Zeus's explanation of his deception as an excuse. She turned Callisto into a bear, to be viciously hunted. Zeus, anxious to save her from death, snatched Callisto away and placed her, with her son, in the heavens as twin constellations, the Great and the Lesser Bear. On another occasion Actaeon, prince of Thebes, who was a follower of Artemis and himself sworn to chastity, accidentally caught sight of the goddess bathing naked while he was hunting in the forest. He was instantly turned into a stag and pursued to the death by his own hounds.

Artemis's concept of chastity was completely different from that of Athena, whose refusal to marry did not in any way alienate her from male company—on the contrary, she seems to have sought it out, taking young heroes under her patronage, and freely involving herself in all the public, and therefore masculine, affairs of mortals, particularly in wars and politics. Artemis, on the other hand, actively repudiated male company, and showed no interest in boy children. Nonetheless, there are stories that suggest that she lapsed occasionally from her austere purity. Some myths maintain that she succumbed to Pan when the ugly but energetic woodland god came to her disguised as a white goat. Also, different reasons are given to explain her shooting of the beautiful giant hunter Orion: some poets claim she did so because she was jealous that he preferred Aurora, goddess of the dawn, although most say it was because he assaulted one of her nymphs or even Artemis herself. He was later transformed into a constellation (see page 80).

It is significant that some myths imply that Artemis had a sensual side to her nature. These stories, as well as Artemis's role as protectress of childbirth, associate her with fertility, in contrast to her main identity as a virgin goddess. Her role as moon goddess also reinforces this connection. Artemis originally had no lunar associations, but as the mythic tradition developed and centered around the Olympian gods, she came to subsume the identity of Selene, a daughter of the Titans, who was the original goddess of the moon. (Similarly, the identity of Helius, the sun god, merged with Apollo, Artemis's twin brother; see page 82.) In addition Artemis partially absorbed the attributes of Hecate, another goddess of the moon and also of ghosts and witchcraft, who resided under the Earth in the realm of Hades. Among Hecate's powers was a measure of control over the fertility of the Earth. This association with a feared sorceress gave a menacing aspect to Artemis's character.

Often the three moon goddesses were depicted as one, and some statues of Artemis showed her with three heads, combining all three aspects of her character. Ovid, the Roman poet, explained that the goddess was called Luna (the moon) in the heavens, Artemis on the Earth, and Hecate in the Underworld. The linked goddesses also symbolized the three phases of the lunar cycle, with Artemis representing the crescent-

This Greek stone relief, *c.* 470 BCE, that once adorned a temple in Asia Minor depicts Actaeon being attacked by his own hunting dogs—acting upon a command from Artemis—after he accidentally saw her bathing naked. The goddess always zealously guarded her chastity.

shaped moon, Selene the full moon and Hecate the phase during which no moon is visible.

Artemis, or Diana to the Romans, was always more popular in the eastern areas of the Mediterranean and in the Aegean islands than in mainland Greece or Italy. Her main temple, at Ephesus in Asia Minor, was considered one of the seven wonders of the ancient world. It remained an important religious site for centuries: in the first century CE Paul of Tarsus caused a riot in Ephesus by trying to preach the Christian faith there. The statue of her in this temple (see page 76) showed her with many breasts and with other symbols connected with fertility goddesses. More usually,

The Gods and the Heavens

Not only Orion, the victim of Artemis's wrath, but also many other mythological characters lent their names to the stars, constellations, and planets.

The Greeks were magnificent astronomers, combining the accumulated wisdom of Mesopotamian, Persian, and Egyptian science with their own keen observations and geometrical calculations, and their work formed the basis for all later Western investigations of the heavens. By the second century CE, the renowned Greek astronomer Ptolemy had catalogued more than one thousand stars, divided into forty-eight constellations.

All the prominent constellations of the northern hemisphere were named by the Greeks, who were sometimes influenced by the symbolism perceived by earlier traditions. Most of the constellations were named after mythological characters or stories: for example, Orion is named for a victim of Artemis's arrows.

The classical astronomers knew of only five planets, other than our own, which were distinguished from the stars because their positions in the heavens were not fixed. The innermost of these, Mercury, moves the fastest, and was therefore named after the fleet-footed messenger of the gods. Venus was the most beautiful Olympian, and her planet is the brightest object (after the sun and the moon) in the heavens, glowing pale and serene at dawn and dusk. Mars is red, the color of war. Jupiter, as the largest, was named after the greatest of the gods. Saturn, the most distant planet visible to the ancients, was identified by the Romans with the Titan Cronus, and was named for the popular agricultural god Saturn, his Roman equivalent. His festival, the Saturnalia, was celebrated when the Sun entered Capricorn, the zodiacal sign governed by Saturn.

The astronomers who named the three planets discovered since then have respected this tradition. Uranus is more distant than Saturn, meaning that the three generations of sky god—Jupiter, Saturn (Cronus), and Uranus—stretch out into the heavens in generational order. Astronomers agreed to name the eighth planet, discovered in the nineteenth century, after Neptune, Jupiter's brother and one of the most illustrious of the Olympian gods. The final planet, discovered in 1930, was named Pluto after the third of the brothers victorious over the Titans.

According to Greek myth, the hunter Orion was turned into a constellation after he was killed by Artemis for having offended her.

however, she was represented as young and tall, wearing a short, practical tunic, carrying a bow and arrow and accompanied by her hounds. Occasionally she drove a chariot drawn by two heifers or horses, each a different color. In rural areas, her statue was sometimes set up at cross-roads: this acknowledged her connection with Hecate, because in popular superstition cross-

sacrifice to Artemis anyone who was shipwrecked on their coast, and legend had it that the Spartans only gave up their annual human sacrifice to her in the reforms of the legendary lawgiver Lycurgus in the ninth century BCE, replacing this ceremony with a ritual of self-flagellation.

The Romans seem to have found Diana, their equivalent to Artemis, less attractive than the rest

roads were often considered to be haunted. As a result of this she came to be known during the Roman period as Diana Trivia—*trivia* being the Latin word for crossroads.

Artemis was associated with human sacrifice (see page 43) for longer than the other Olympian gods, and this connection may in part account for the element of fear and loathing that was some-times attached to her name. The people of the Tauric Chersonese on the Black Sea were said to

On this 7th-century BCE set of gold pectoral plaques, Artemis is depicted in her guise as Mistress of Animals. She was the goddess of the woods and wild places.

of their imported pantheon, despite the fact that she was sister to Apollo, one of their most impor-tant gods. Juno, the Roman form of Hera, took over many of her responsibilities toward women and children, and religious devotion to her conse-quently declined.

81

Apollo, God of Light

The twin brother of Artemis, Apollo was the god of light, and of the sun itself, but he was also the patron of music, poetry, and all the fine arts, and of healing and prophecy. Although he was a figure of great beauty, and a favored subject of artists and sculptors, he was often unhappy in love.

Apollo, the younger twin born to Zeus and Leto, attracted none of the jealous punishment that Hera usually wreaked on her husband's illegitimate offspring. He was always an imposing figure on Olympus, and Zeus entrusted him with the power of knowing the future.

Just as Artemis took on the attributes of Selene, the moon goddess, so Apollo came to appropriate the qualities of Helius, god of the sun (see page 28). He was commonly called Phoebus Apollo—*phoibos*, meaning bright, was the epithet originally applied to Helius. This synthesis of two myths led to some confusion. The sun was seen in mythology as a fiery chariot pulled by two flying horses, which the sun god drove daily across the sky. But although he was regarded as the sun god, Apollo was never thought to perform this task. Instead it continued to be carried out by Helius, who maintained a separate identity from Apollo. This stands as an example of how the Greeks, in particular, could happily accept contradictions within their mythology.

Stories of Apollo's childhood and upbringing are rare. It is told that, as an infant, he shot the serpent-monster Python (see page 35), who had been torturing his mother at the behest of Hera. By killing it he gained possession of the oracular site at Delphi, where the monster had dwelled. Apollo lived on Olympus and was usually highly honored by Zeus, although they quarrelled bitterly when Apollo killed a she-dragon sacred to

Apollo and his twin sister Diana (Artemis) are shown decorating a sacred pillar, in this terra-cotta plaque from the Temple of Apollo on the Palatine hill in Rome.

The Sacred Oracle

From as early as the third millennium BCE, Delphi was an important sacred site. The Greeks dedicated the complex to Apollo, and it was believed that the god himself spoke there through the mouth of his priestess, the Pythia.

The importance of this oracle can hardly be exaggerated. It was a major center of the Greek world, unifying the city-states. In addition, it drew visitors, many of them rulers, from all over the Mediterranean and the Middle East. Delphi came to be regarded as the geographical center of the universe and was often called "the navel of the world": a sacred stone known as the *omphalos* (navel) was located in the sanctuary. This stone was said to have been the one given by Rhea to Cronus to swallow in place of the infant Zeus (see page 30).

A complex ritual developed at Delphi. Anyone who wanted to know their destiny made offerings of a sacred cake and a goat or a sheep, before consulting the Pythia, the priestess of the shrine.

After careful purification she sat on a tripod, a bowl on three legs, and fell into a trance-like state in which she received answers from Apollo. When she spoke, her words were copied down by a group of priests who then interpreted them and delivered the results to the supplicant. When the message of the god was negative, the Pythia refused to speak at all. Sometimes the prophecies at Delphi were ambiguous. Croesus, emperor of Lydia, consulted the oracle when considering a campaign against Persia and was told that he would destroy a great empire— he did, but unfortunately it was his own. More often they were extremely obscure, or open to almost any meaning.

Despite difficulties of interpretation, the oracle at Delphi was regarded as authoritative. It was consulted by anyone seeking guidance on major affairs of state, military expeditions, or religious or moral issues. Around the cave a large complex of temples, treasuries, and hostels developed, with a great arena for the important Pythian Games, which were founded in 582 BCE. Colonnaded walks displayed statues of gods and heroes that had been donated in Apollo's honor.

Delphi's importance both as an oracle and as a social focus began to wane in the third century BCE, as the Greek world expanded. In Roman times, its popularity was overtaken by other forms of augury, such as the skilled interpretation of dreams, weather patterns or the flight of birds.

The sacred oracle at Delphi was built at the base of Mount Parnassus, one of the most spectacular locations in Greece.

Gaia. Because of this, Apollo was exiled from Olympus and was forced to live for nine years on Earth. There he became a shepherd to Admetus, king of Thessaly, whom he later rewarded with immortality because he had proved such a generous employer. Apollo was known as the god of shepherds, and for this reason a wolf, the scourge of shepherds, was often sacrificed to him.

Apollo was commonly known as the god of music. Many representations show him with the lyre, the hand-held, seven-stringed musical instrument popular with the Greeks, and particularly important because it was used to accompany performances of poetry. Apollo had obtained the lyre from Hermes (see page 101), who invented it, and became immensely skilled at playing the instrument; he also instructed mortals in its use.

He was proud of his musical ability. Marsyas, a satyr, once challenged him to a competition, claiming that the music of his flute was sweeter than Apollo's lyre. After the Muses, the judges in this competition, declared Apollo the winner, he had Marsyas flayed alive for his impertinence. On another occasion he inflicted donkey's ears on King Midas for daring to prefer Pan's pipes to his lyre. But he could also use his musical gifts on behalf of humanity. For example, he assisted Poseidon in the founding of Troy, playing his lyre so sweetly that city walls seemed to grow to the sound of his music.

Like the other Olympians, Apollo was frequently involved in love affairs, many of which ended unhappily. He was unfaithful to the nymph Clytia, who pined to death and was reborn as the sunflower, always turning her face toward the sun, her lost lover. Daphne was so desperate to

This Etruscan terra-cotta figure of Apollo, known as the Apollo of Veii, was crafted in the 5th century BCE. It is one of the oldest Roman representations of the Greek gods. With its fixed eyes and blank smile, the statue was fashioned in a style reminiscent of very early Greek figures.

escape his amorous advances that she had herself turned into a laurel tree (see page 131), which is why Apollo was always associated with that plant. In an attempt to seduce Cassandra, princess of Troy, Apollo rashly gave her the gift of prophecy. Although she still rejected him, he could not take back the gift, so he punished her by ordaining that nobody would ever believe her truthful prophecies. When she foretold the fall of Troy during the Trojan War, her own people assumed she was mad and refused to heed her warnings.

Apollo's authority was tremendous and stemmed in part from his role as the god of divination. His temple and shrine at Delphi were the most famous in the Mediterranean world, but he had numerous other oracles. His two mottos, "Know yourself" and "Nothing in excess," which were carved on a gateway there, reflected the Greek philosophy of life. His male beauty also epitomized a Greek ideal.

Apollo was the only Olympian god whose name was not changed when he was adopted into the Roman pantheon. Rather than being gradually merged with local Italian gods, he was introduced suddenly, in response to an oracle following an epidemic. He was respected by the Romans for his role as a healer but was never as prominent among them as he was among the Greeks.

Asclepius, the Healer

Apollo's gift of healing was inherited by one of his sons, Asclepius, who was so skilled a doctor that after his death he was transformed into the god of medicine.

Apollo's lover, Coronis, was unfaithful to him, even though she was pregnant. For this, he exacted fierce revenge: he burned her to death with lightning but rescued the child from her womb and sent him to be educated by Chiron, the wise centaur.

Apollo's son Asclepius became a healer, and was regarded as the inventor of medicine itself; he was physician to the Argonauts on their great journey to Colchis. So great was his skill that he began to restore the dead to life. Hades, offended, complained to Zeus, who punished Asclepius's presumption by killing

Asclepius is shown exercising his legendary healing powers on a Greek man who is identified as Archinus on this 4th-century BCE relief.

him with a thunderbolt during Apollo's nine-year exile from Olympus. When Apollo returned, he gave Asclepius divine status as the god of medicine.

His principal temple was at Epidaurus, but he also had many others throughout the classical world. The Romans built him a major shrine after their city was delivered from a plague. His temples were equipped with gymnasia and baths, and while many of the recorded cures were miraculous, others were probably due to the priests' knowledge of herbal remedies and sound therapeutic regimens.

85

Hephaestus, the Heavenly Craftsman

Hephaestus, the god of forges and of metalwork, was neither beautiful nor awe-inspiring and was frequently the victim of savage teasing by the other gods. Yet the products of his workshop were magnificent and perfectly suited to their purpose.

The classical mythographers told two very different stories about Hephaestus's birth and parentage. Some writers said that because Hera was envious of Zeus for producing a child, Athena, from his own head, she thought she would emulate this feat by having a child herself without any procreative act. However, when her son Hephaestus was born, she was so disappointed by his ugliness that she threw him out of Olympus, crippling him as he crashed on Earth.

Other accounts say that he was the son of Hera and Zeus, and was born normal and healthy like the other gods. As he grew up, he began to take his mother's side in her marital squabbles. One day Zeus, infuriated by Hera's interference and insolence, decided to teach her a lesson by suspending her from the ceiling of their palace by a golden chain. But Hephaestus released her, angering Zeus, who then hurled his son out of Olympus. Hephaestus fell for nine days, finally landing on the island of Lemnos. He broke his leg so badly when he hit the Earth that he was lame for the rest of his life. On Lemnos he was welcomed and honored by the inhabitants, so he built himself a palace and smithy there, and the island became his home. The people of Lemnos learned from him and became famous metalworkers themselves.

Hephaestus, god of forges and metalwork, is shown hard at work in his smithy in this lively detail from a 5th-century BCE Greek drinking cup.

His reconciliation with the family of Olympian gods resulted from one of Hephaestus's magnificent creations. He constructed a handsome golden throne, which he offered as a gift to his mother, Hera. However, the throne was designed to punish Hera for her lack of affection. As soon as she sat on it, she was trapped by a secret mechanism and was unable to move. All the powers of the other Olympian gods could not release her. Dionysus, god of wine, was sent to Lemnos to try to restore good relations. He got Hephaestus, his half-brother, extremely drunk and was able to persuade him to return to Olympus. Here Hephaestus not only liberated his mother but also was reconciled with his family. Although he chose to continue spending his time on Lemnos—or, according to the Romans, on the island of Sicily where the active volcano of Mount Etna provided him with a forge—he was thereafter a frequent visitor to the other gods on Olympus.

Hephaestus created many valuable items for both gods and men. Among the most impressive was Pandora, the first woman, whom some say he made at Zeus's request as part of the punishment of Prometheus (see page 37). With the Cyclopes, who were often represented as his assistants, he also made Zeus's famous thunderbolts. He was particularly fond of creating automata, including the magical golden furniture of Olympus, which could move itself in and out of rooms.

Despite his ugliness Hephaestus had a number of children, although most of them inherited, in one form or another, some of their father's deformities. He fathered Cecrops, the reputed founder of Athens, who was said to be human above his waist and below it to have the body of a snake. Cacus, the son of Hephaestus and Medusa, the Gorgon, had three heads and continually vomited fire, and grew up to become an infamous robber.

Promised by Zeus that he could marry the goddess of his choice, Hephaestus selected Athena, but she defended her chastity fiercely. He eventually wedded Aphrodite, but this marriage between the goddess of beauty and the deformed god was not successful.

The Romans revered Hephaestus more than the Greeks did, honoring him under the name of Vulcan. Roman poets placed his principal home in Sicily, but saw his presence everywhere in volcanoes and volcanic activity. This link was broadened into an association with fire in general, which is a creative as well as a destructive force. Metalworking, including smelting and forging, was regarded as a magical or divine activity, because of its central role in the development of civilization. But at the same time, skill in metalworking was

Weapons of the Gods

The Olympian gods are frequently shown bearing arms that were crafted for them by Hephaestus. These arms had a symbolic rather than warlike purpose—after the defeat of the Titans, the Olympians ceased to fight in wars themselves.

Hephaestus forged the thunderbolts of Zeus, which were carried directly from his smithy by an eagle—they arrived just in time to swing the battle of the gods in favor of the Olympians. He also made Hades' helmet of invisibility, Athena's shield and buckler, and Hermes' *talaria*, or winged sandals. The gods lent all these items to the hero Perseus, enabling him to slay Medusa, the Gorgon (see page 125).

Hephaestus also made gifts for favored mortals, usually the sons of the gods. Such was his love for his wife, Aphrodite, that he even forged arms for her illegitimate son, Aeneas. Thetis, the mother of the great Greek hero Achilles, promised Hephaestus favors in exchange for a full suit of armor for her son, although she ultimately refused to honor the agreement. At the request of Zeus he made a shield for Heracles. All these weapons had special powers, derived in part from their divine workmanship, and thus enhanced Hephaestus's reputation.

Each of the Olympian gods had his or her characteristic weaponry, often decorated with their emblems. According to the myth, Athena was born fully armed, and was frequently so depicted. Her shield was often decorated with an owl, symbolizing her wisdom. The bird atop her helmet is a cockerel, another one of her emblems (see page 73).

perceived as being potentially dangerous: the people with the best and strongest weapons tended to be victorious in war and more secure in peacetime. Some experts have suggested that in the ancient Greek and Roman popular imagination, Hephaestus's lameness and his occasional foolishness compensated in some way for his creative genius and his formidable skill: the ability both to make deadly weapons and to use them effectively would represent too much power for one being, even a god.

In the forms of his worship, Hephaestus is set apart from the other Olympians. Sacrifices to him followed a different pattern from those to other gods. In particular, it was customary to burn the whole of his sacrificial animal, rather than keeping some back for the worshippers to feast on after the rite, as was the common practice with such offerings to the other Olympians. In art, he was frequently represented looking more mundane than other gods, often bathed in sweat, with a hairy chest or disheveled hair. He was also depicted in active poses at work in his forge, with his hammer raised above his head, while other divinities generally are shown standing serenely or sitting regally on their thrones.

The Snare of Hephaestus

Hephaestus was married to Aphrodite, but they were ill matched, and she was continually unfaithful to him. Ares, god of war, was her lover in Olympus, and they conducted their affair so blatantly that Hephaestus was driven to seek revenge.

Venus (Aphrodite), Mars (Ares) and Cupid in a 1st-century CE wall painting from Pompeii. Venus and Mars were popular subjects for Roman artists.

When Ares and Aphrodite spent the night together, a young servant, Alectryon, was stationed at the door to warn them of anyone approaching. One night, however, he fell asleep and Apollo, arriving on Olympus at dawn, caught them and reported their behavior to Hephaestus. Enraged by his servant's negligence, Ares turned Alectryon into a rooster, eternally crying out plaintively at the approach of dawn.

Meanwhile Hephaestus, angry and humiliated, returned to Lemnos and set to work. He forged a magical net with a secret spring, which he suspended over his wife's bed. When the couple decided to risk another night of passion, they triggered Hephaestus's net, which fell on them from above, trapping them naked and entwined.

Not content with merely catching them *in flagrante*, Hephaestus summoned the other gods to laugh at his wife's shame. Yet even this elaborate practical joke had painful consequences for Hephaestus. Aphrodite's beauty so enchanted the male gods that they were inclined to take her side rather than that of her injured husband, and to envy rather than despise Ares.

Ares, God of War

Ares, the son of Zeus and Hera, was less popular among the Greeks than the other Olympians, and he had fewer temples, stories, or festivals devoted to him. It was only under the Romans, whose attitude to war was more aggressive, that he rose to prominence, becoming the principal patron of the city of Rome.

Although Ares was one of the Olympian gods, the Greeks felt a certain ambivalence toward him because they did not relish the idea of war, his area of patronage. This is revealed in the disparaging stories they told about him. For example, although he was god of warfare, Ares was captured by the enemy early on in the conflict with the Titans and was imprisoned for fifteen months, until Hermes was able to rescue him. During the Trojan War, in which he sided with the Trojans against the Greeks, he was actually wounded by a mortal, Diomedes, although as a war god he should have epitomized military skill.

Greek artists showed him sometimes as young and fit but more often as an old man, naked and armed with a helmet, shield, and pike. He was attended by retainers such as Discord, Strife, and Panic; the two untameable horses that pulled his chariot were called Flight and Terror. His altars were kept permanently blood-strewn. Horses and wolves were sacred to him, as were magpies and vultures because of their greed.

Ares is the only Olympian god who substantially changed character and function when the Romans adopted the Greek pantheon. For the Romans, war was considered less chaotic and dangerous, and therefore its god was more civilized and a great deal more friendly than the Greek original. They adopted him, as Mars, early on. This was partly because of their own military ardor and successful campaigns of conquest and colonization, but also because Roman mythology was constructed to express its continuity with earlier traditions, and so traced all its founding heroes back to Troy, which Ares had supported. The Romans believed, moreover, that their city had been founded by Romulus, who was held to be a son of Mars, and who, with his twin brother Remus, had been reared by a wolf, an animal sacred to the god. Not surprisingly, Mars was consistently depicted as young and attractive by the Romans.

The Romans associated Mars not just with war, but also with agriculture. Two possible explanations

This 1st- or 2nd-century CE Roman statue, known as the Ares Ludovisi, contrasts the masculinity of Mars with the vulnerability of the baby playing at his feet.

When they depicted him in full armor, as in this bronze statuette of the 2nd or 3rd century CE, the Romans were usually presenting Mars in his role as protector of the state. When shown as guardian of gladiators and athletes, the god would be portrayed naked.

have been advanced for this dual role. Because he was the god of war, Mars may have been asked by his worshippers to protect their fields—against both spiritual and physical enemies. Alternatively, some Roman myths suggest that he may have originally been an Italian agricultural god who only later took on the role of god of war. In these stories, his origins are related to the power of nature: for example, Flora, the Roman goddess of flowering plants, was said to have given Juno (the Roman Hera) a flower that enabled her to conceive Mars on her own; and his consort was sometimes an Italian fertility goddess, Neiro.

Many Italian cities named the month of March, or *Martius*, after him—falling at the beginning of the spring, it was typically a time when prayers were offered for the growth of crops. Most of his festivals took place at this time, although others were held in October, during the harvest. Roman military campaigns were often launched in the spring, and for this reason several of the March festivals included militaristic activities.

Mars's importance to the Romans was demonstrated by the fact that his priests were entrusted with the Ancile, one of the most sacred treasures of Rome. It was a holy shield that was said to have fallen from heaven to protect the city from plague. So anxious were the Romans to preserve the Ancile that they had eleven exact copies made to confuse any would-be thief. One of the most important religious festivals of Rome was a procession in honor of Mars, when the Ancile and its copies were carried around the city walls by his priests as they danced and sang his praises. This celebration lasted three days, from March 1, and during this time business was suspended.

The most famous temple of Mars was built in Rome by Augustus to celebrate his victory at Philippi in 42 BCE. Before setting out on any expedition, the consul, and later the emperor, would offer prayers at the temple. Then, in a solemn ritual, he would shake the spear in the hand of the god's statue and commend the whole city to his protection with the words: "God of War, watch over the safety of this city."

Dionysus, God of the Grape

Dionysus (or Bacchus), the god of wine, the grape harvest and fermentation, as well as of altered states and drunkenness, is sometimes seen as a latecomer to Olympus, where he is thought to have ousted either Hermes (see pages 100–103) or Hestia (see page 105) to claim his place among the twelve Olympians. Whereas the myths and religious practices of the other gods tended to promote civic order, Dionysus pursued a wild and dangerous path of his own.

Of all the members of the Olympian family, Dionysus alone was said to have a mortal parent. In some myths, Zeus was his father, and his mother was Semele, a princess of Thebes. As the daughter of Cadmus and Harmony, she had already aroused the enmity of Hera, because Cadmus's sister, Europa, had been loved by Zeus (see page 47). So when Zeus became enamoured of Semele and made her pregnant, Hera not surprisingly inflicted on her the full force of her jealous wrath. The revenge she devised was both subtle and terrible. Disguising herself as Semele's old nurse, she visited the princess and persuaded her that she should insist on receiving proof of Zeus's divine identity by asking him to appear before her in his glory. Semele first extracted a promise from Zeus that he would grant her any request, and then demanded that he reveal his true self to her. No mortal could bear such a sight, but equally no god could retract

a promise. When Zeus manifested himself in his full radiance before his mistress, she immediately burst into flames and was burned to ashes. However, her unborn child was rescued, some say by Zeus himself: the god sewed him into his thigh and thus kept him safe until he was mature enough to be born. Other versions claim that the child was snatched from the fire by the god Hermes or by a nymph, Dirce.

This story of Dionysus's origins differs significantly from another version that refers to him fighting alongside the other Olympians against the Titans. His human mother, Semele, could not have existed during this early period in the history of the world. In this account Dionysus was the child of Zeus and Persephone. Jealous Hera incited the Titans to attack the boy: they chopped him into pieces, but he was regenerated, either by his own power or with Zeus's assistance.

The theme of rebirth is echoed in another story in which Dionysus journeys to the

This statue of Bacchus (Dionysus) is a Roman copy of a Greek original that dates from after the time of Alexander the Great. Images of the god often have a touch of effeminacy, in contrast to the more masculine deities such as Apollo and Ares.

Bacchic Rites

The practices of the cult of Dionysus included dancing, singing, and ecstatic shouting and could easily tip over into manic and demented behavior. Members of the cult stressed the joy and emotional release that this god offered his followers.

Although wine flowed in honor of the god of the vine, the Dionysiac orgy also had a religious aim—to burst through social restraints into a world of divine, chaotic freedom and abandonment. In Athens, the rituals of Dionysus were first celebrated with public solemnity. They involved the participation of the chief magistrate of the city, and the priests in charge of the rituals were given honored seats at public games.

The Dionysia, or Bacchanalia, were public festivals of mirth. People dressed up as characters from the myths of Dionysus. Some, for example, appeared as satyrs, draped in skins and with ivy or vine garlands around their heads, and each carried a *thursos*, a wand made of fennel wrapped with vines and topped with ivy. Virgins carried baskets of fruit in which snakes were hidden, because followers were believed to have the power to charm snakes. Some men dressed as women, and others carried sticks. Participants imitated drunks and lunatics, played noisy music and copied the maddened howls of the mythical followers of the god, known as Bacchantes.

However, there were also mysteries of which the cult's initiates were forbidden to speak. In myth—and perhaps in reality—these involved dismembering live animals and eating their flesh raw. Rumor embroidered this into stories of human sacrifice and cannibalism. The cultic priestesses were said to preside naked except for wildflower garlands, and to indulge in acts of gross indecency. Above all there were consistent reports of orgies, drunkenness, and debauchery. People in Greece and Rome believed that Dionysus incited his devotees to wildness, through both drink and religious fervor, until they could no longer control themselves and might commit murder or rape.

This Roman 1st-century CE relief depicts three revellers enjoying a Bacchic procession.

Underworld to bring his mother, Semele, back to life. This reference to Dionysus's power in the Underworld struck a chord, and in the religious cult of Dionysus, his followers were promised an eternal afterlife of drinking and pleasure.

Mythographers are generally in agreement about the god's upbringing, saying that Dionysus was educated by nymphs and grew in divine power as he matured. According to a popular tale, the young Dionysus was kidnapped as he slept by pirates or merchant sailors who planned to sell him into slavery. When he awoke he was outraged and punished his captors. First he becalmed the boat in which he was taken captive by entwining the rigging with vines, and then he turned all the crew (except the pilot, who had shown some remorse) into dolphins—it is said that they continue to follow ships in the hope that they will be converted back into human form.

The most common theme in stories about Dionysus concerns his mysterious journey from the East. These tales have led some scholars to believe that originally he may have been imported into Greece from Thrace or from Phrygia in Asia Minor, where his worship was always strong. He was said to have led an army—consisting of men, women and children, together with satyrs and maenads—that conquered all the peoples with whom it came into contact, using only peaceful means. The tribes that the army confronted were only too happy to be introduced to the pleasures of wine and the technique of fermentation. Dionysus also taught the art of crop cultivation and the skills of beekeeping.

In art, Dionysus is usually represented as young and effeminate. He shares Apollo's youth and long hair, but while Apollo's locks are golden, Dionysus's are usually dark, and he is always plumper. Images of him are often less dignified: for example, he is frequently illustrated naked, carried on the shoulders of his companions. Sometimes he is depicted as a chubby child, holding a bunch of grapes and blowing on a trumpet.

Dionysus was not simply a god of drunkenness and pleasure. He was also an important fertility god, crucial to the life-cycle of vegetation, to farming and arboriculture. Many of the gods of the countryside or woodland belonged to his band of followers. Pan, for example, was his servant and companion; Silenus, a wise demi-god of the pastures, was his teacher and devoted counselor; and in the army that marched west were many of the nature spirits from the oldest branches of classical mythology (see page 55).

Seen predominantly as generous and benevolent, Dionysus rewarded services lavishly. He was also sympathetic. He married Ariadne, whom he brought back to life after she had hanged herself when her first husband Theseus deserted her on the island of Naxos. Dionysus and she had many children together, and the god was regarded as having been predominantly faithful to

A Greek terra-cotta dish from the 4th century BCE shows the young Dionysus in a boat after he had been kidnapped by sailors. Surrounding the boat are his captors, who were changed into dolphins as punishment.

her—unlike the other Olympians, he was not spectacularly promiscuous or lecherous. One of his few illegitimate children, whom he conceived with Aphrodite, was Hymenaeus, a god of marriage; despite his illicit liaison, Dionysus continued to represent fidelity.

At the same time, Dionysus was known to deal out savage punishments to those he felt had offended him, or who disbelieved in his divine status. When Lycurgus, king of Thrace, forbade the worship of Dionysus, refused to allow his subjects to cultivate vines and tried to expel the god and his followers from his kingdom, Dionysus drove him mad. In a demented fury, Lycurgus put his son Dryas to death and then hacked off his own legs, believing them to be vine boughs. He was ultimately tortured to death by his subjects, who were told by an oracle that they would not taste wine again while he lived.

Pentheus's fate, as recounted in *The Bacchae*, a play by the fifth-century BCE tragedian Euripides, was perhaps even more horrible, partly because Pentheus was a close relation of Dionysus. He was the nephew of Semele, the mother of Dionysus, and thus the god's first cousin. As the king of Thebes, Pentheus found the

newly introduced orgiastic rites of Dionysus offensive, despite (or because of) their great popularity with the women of his city. He forbade the rites and attempted to arrest Dionysus when he came to Thebes to foster his cult. No prison built by mortals could contain the god, however, and after walking free, Dionysus led his devoted followers up into the mountains above Thebes to celebrate. In a rage Pentheus gave an order to his troops to execute every worshipper, but this was not carried out. Indignant at his cousin's lack of respect, Dionysus implanted in his mind an overwhelming curiosity to see what the secret rituals involved.

The cult of Bacchus was particularly popular among women. These worshippers are shown on a Roman carving from the 1st century CE.

The king hid among the trees to watch the revellers, who were driven mad by the ecstasies of the cult. When they found Pentheus spying on them, the revelers—led by his own mother and two aunts—tore him to pieces with their bare hands.

The idea that Dionysus had the power to drive mortals to insanity often frightened officials who were responsible for law and order, and the fact that his rites were particularly popular with women only increased the level of public disquiet. Greek literature records frequent complaints that the Dionysian orgies were corrupting the manners and morals of all classes. And in Rome, in the second century BCE, the orgies reached such scandalous proportions, taking place around five times a month, that the Senate ordered a complete ban on them and other related cultic activities, in an uncharacteristic act of religious censorship.

Nonetheless it proved impossible to stamp out devotion to Dionysus. Around 100 years after the Senate ban, mystery religions—secretive cults that offered highly personal and sometimes ecstatic religious experiences—began to flourish openly again. Dionysian cults, among others, thrived until Christianity became the official state religion and such practices were again suppressed.

Midas and the Touch of Gold

Dionysus was as generous to those who honored him as he was ferocious to those who insulted him. He gave lavish rewards, but could not always guarantee that their effects would be beneficial—as the famous story of Midas, king of Phrygia, illustrates.

One day some peasants brought to King Midas Silenus, an old friend and teacher of Dionysus, who was so drunk that he had fallen asleep in a garden. Midas took care of him, entertained him, and returned him to the god. Dionysus was so grateful that he promised Midas anything he wished as a reward.

Midas requested that everything he touched might be turned to gold. Dionysus warned him against this choice, but granted the wish as he had promised. Midas plucked the branch of a tree and was thrilled to find a perfect golden bough in his hand; he then created a golden stone, a glittering apple, and sandal straps of pure gold. Too soon, however, he realized the foolishness of his choice. He could not eat, because the bread became solid gold in his hand; he could not drink because the liquid turned to gold in his mouth. Even his beloved daughter was transformed into cold metal when she affectionately embraced him.

Desperate and humbled, he begged Dionysus to take away his gift, and the god consented. He told Midas to bathe in the Pactolus River. The magic power passed from the king to the river, and now the sands of the Pactolus sparkle with pure gold.

The Greeks had great respect for gold and silver and considered metalwork an art. Most reliefs in precious metals, such as these 4th-century BCE Thracian silver and gold panels, were created for religious sanctuaries.

A Family Tree of the Gods and Goddesses

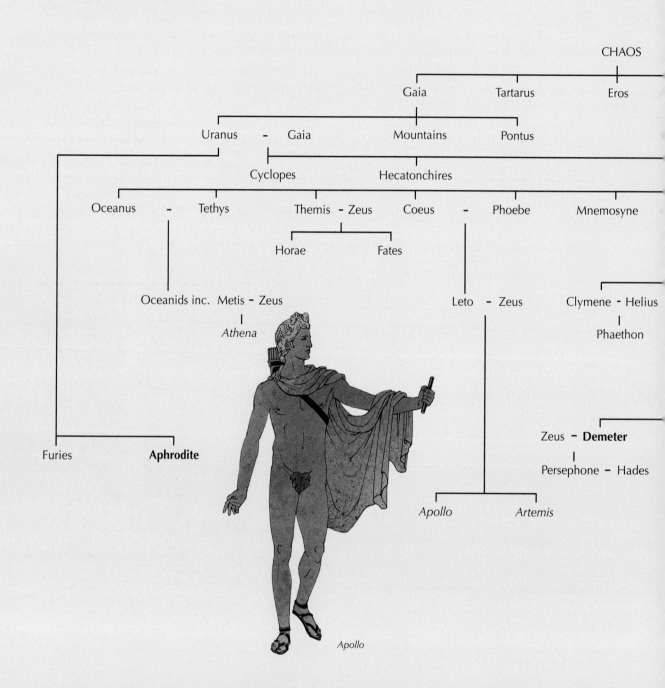

CHAOS

Gaia — Tartarus — Eros

Uranus - Gaia — Mountains — Pontus

Cyclopes — Hecatonchires

Oceanus - Tethys — Themis - Zeus — Coeus - Phoebe — Mnemosyne

Horae — Fates

Oceanids inc. Metis - Zeus — Leto - Zeus — Clymene - Helius

Athena — Phaethon

Zeus - **Demeter**

Persephone - Hades

Furies — **Aphrodite** — Apollo — Artemis

Apollo

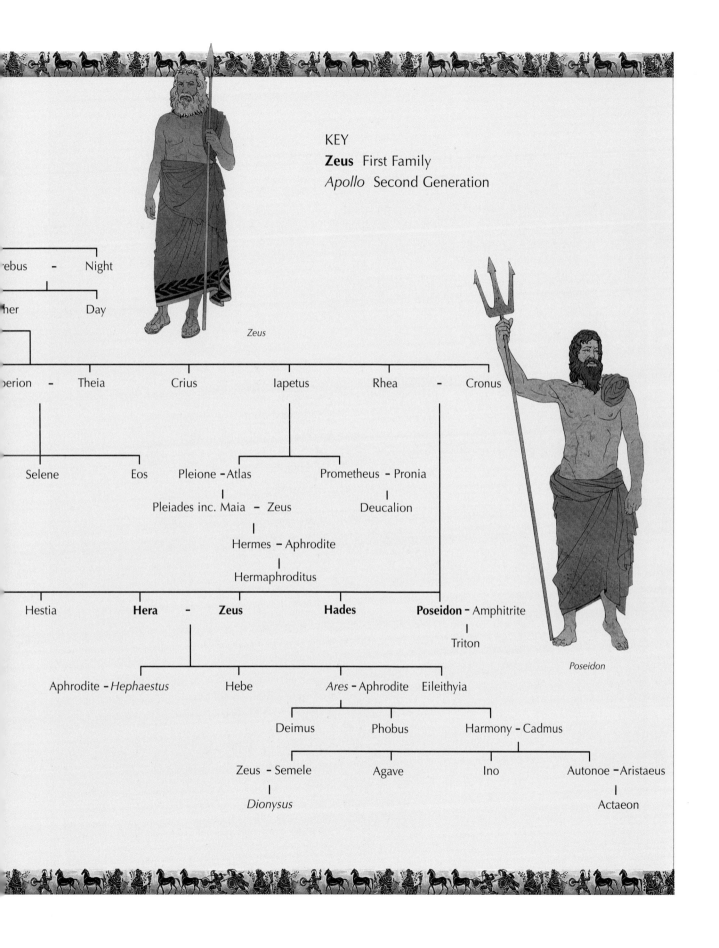

KEY
Zeus First Family
Apollo Second Generation

rebus – Night

her Day

berion – Theia   Crius   Iapetus   Rhea – Cronus

Selene   Eos   Pleione – Atlas   Prometheus – Pronia

Pleiades inc. Maia – Zeus   Deucalion

Hermes – Aphrodite

Hermaphroditus

Hestia   **Hera** – **Zeus**   **Hades**   **Poseidon** – Amphitrite

Triton

Aphrodite – *Hephaestus*   Hebe   *Ares* – Aphrodite   Eileithyia

Deimus   Phobus   Harmony – Cadmus

Zeus – Semele   Agave   Ino   Autonoe – Aristaeus

Dionysus   Actaeon

Zeus

Poseidon

GODS AND THE LIFE OF HUMANKIND

However enthralling their triumphs and feuds, the supreme Olympian gods remained remote from the reality of people's everyday lives. Even the festivals in their honor, which brought citizens together in collective worship, were civic occasions more than opportunities for personal communion.

It was therefore hardly surprising that ordinary mortals should feel special affection for the handful of divinities whose concerns somehow seemed to touch on their own mundane realities. For example, they had a soft spot for Hermes, a god with whom they could identify. As the patron of thieves and others who lived on their wits, he was less unapproachably lofty than his fellow deities. His Roman equivalent, Mercury, was so popular that his statue became a common garden ornament.

People were also fascinated by lesser deities who were thought to have a direct influence on their own well-being. Some were personified abstractions, like Tyche, goddess of luck or chance, and her Roman counterpart, Fortuna. Others, including the dreaded Nemesis, punished wrong-doers. Most important of all were the Fates—the three goddesses known as the Moirae in Greece and the Parcae in Rome; even today, there are people in Greece who believe that these goddesses visit newborn infants to allot them their pre-ordained destiny.

While Greeks in search of individual religious experience often turned to mystery cults, the more practically minded Romans also worshipped a range of domestic gods whose natural habitat was the home. Each household had its own *lares,* spirits of dead ancestors, and *penates*, who guaranteed food in the store cupboard. And Vesta, the virgin goddess of the hearth, was a beneficent presence honored both in homes and in temples, who ensured well-being for all who won her favor.

One aspect of religion that concerned every individual, Greek and Roman alike, was the soul's fate after death. The poets responded with visions of the Underworld whose imaginative power can be felt to this day. But people who were anxious about their own mortality found little comfort in these chilling visions; and as the classical era drew to a close, they turned instead to mystery religions and other faiths that held out greater hope of consolation.

Above: This 3rd-century CE embossed votive leaf depicts Mercury, the Roman equivalent of the popular and down-to-earth Greek god Hermes.

Opposite: Pan, half-man, half-goat, was a god of the woodlands, who made beautiful music on his pipes. On this Roman jug, he plays for a Maenad, a follower of Dionysus.

Hermes, Fleet of Foot

God of flocks and boundaries, of travelers, traders, and thieves, Hermes was also a divine messenger, a trickster and the Psychopomp, the conductor of dead souls to the Underworld. His tasks were so various that ancient authors sometimes wondered if more than one deity might shelter under his name.

Hermes was said to have been born on Mount Kyllene, the highest point in the northern Peloponnese in Greece. His father was Zeus and his mother the goddess Maia, daughter of Atlas who held up the world.

The god was precocious as a baby. On the morning of his birth, he crawled out of the cave where his mother was sheltering and came upon a tortoise. Looking at it, he had the idea of using the shell as the sounding-board of a musical instrument. After killing the creature he added two arms, a cross-piece and strings to its shell, and so invented the first lyre.

He wandered on until he came to Pieria in northern Greece. Seeing a herd of well-fed cattle grazing in a meadow, he decided to steal fifty of the beasts. Born cunning, he plotted to conceal the deed: he led the cattle away backward, and made large sandals out of bark for himself to disguise his own footprints. Then he hurried them home, stopping only to kill and eat a couple of the cows, piously sacrificing some of the meat.

The cattle were the prized possessions of Apollo, and the sun god was furious to learn of his loss. He traveled all over Greece looking for the missing beasts and eventually offered a reward for information. Some versions of the myth say it was Silenus and his satyrs who led Apollo to Maia's cave, others that it was the flight of a divinatory bird. Either way, arriving at the cave and finding some familiar cow hides stretched nearby, Apollo at once accused the innocent-looking infant of the

In this early Greek relief, Hermes is shown carrying a ram, symbolizing his role as a pastoral god. He was also frequently depicted holding a shepherd's staff.

theft. At first his mother Maia did not believe him, but Apollo persisted in his accusations. Eventually Zeus was forced to intervene, and Hermes had to confess and return the cattle.

To soothe Apollo's anger, the baby started playing tunes on the lyre he had invented. Apollo was so entranced by the beauty of the sound that when the infant offered to give him the instrument as compensation, he forgave him, and the two became firm friends. In return for the lyre, Apollo offered Hermes the shepherd's staff that was to become his symbol. Known as the *caduceus*, it was represented in later years with two snakes entwined around it.

That was the mythical account of Hermes' babyhood. His name actually had a more mundane origin. It derives from the word *herma*, a rock-pile or cairn used to mark roads and frontiers, an apt name for the god of travelers and boundaries. In paintings and sculptures he was often shown as an adult wearing the short cape, broad-brimmed hat and sandals favored by Greeks on voyages. In his case, however, the hat and sandals had wings, given by Zeus to speed him on his way.

Among the Olympians, Hermes's role was to act as messenger of the gods, helping to put their plans into action. For example, in the Judgement

Divine Music

Music in Greek myth was associated with the pastoral gods, Hermes, Apollo, and Pan. Hermes invented the lyre, and Apollo became its greatest exponent. Pan, the woodland god, created a musical instrument of his own.

Like all the satyrs, who were half man and half goat as he was, the god Pan adored music, dancing, and beautiful women. He fell passionately in love with a nymph named Syrinx, but his appearance terrified her and she fled from him. The god was about to catch up with her when the desperate nymph sent a prayer to Gaia, Mother Earth. To Pan's dismay, Gaia rescued her by instantly transforming her into a clump of reeds.

Distraught, the frustrated lover threw himself down among the plants, sighing deeply. The reeds caught his breath and amplified it plaintively. Intrigued, Pan picked seven reeds of differing lengths and bound them

together. So was born the instrument the Greeks called *syrinx* but which is now known as the Pan pipes.

Although the Greeks delighted in music, it often had tragic associations in their myths. The satyr Marsyas, who challenged the god Apollo to a musical contest and lost, was flayed alive for his arrogance (see page 84). And King Midas (see page 95), who had the bad taste to prefer the music of Pan to that of the sun god in a similar competition, was punished by Apollo with a pair of ass's ears.

One of the Muses plays a lyre on this Greek vase from *c.* 440 BCE.

The Wanderings of Io

In the story of Zeus's affair with Io, Hermes plays a typical role, stepping in to help the god out of a difficult situation. The story may reflect myths of Hathor, the cow-headed goddess of the ancient Egyptians, which were brought back to Greece by early travelers.

Io, a priestess of Hera, had been seduced by Zeus, like many beautiful mortals. Hera herself came upon the couple one day as they dallied in a meadow. Desperate to hide his infidelity, Zeus turned his lover into a heifer, hoping that the harmless-looking beast would escape his wife's jealous attention. But Hera at once suspected trickery, and insisted on taking the animal for herself. She entrusted it for safe-keeping to her monstrous servant, the hundred-eyed Argus, who was said never to close all his eyes at once.

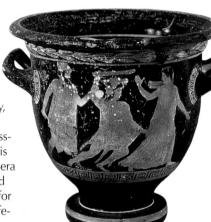

Io watches Hermes kill the hundred-eyed Argus: a Greek vase decoration.

To recover his mistress, Zeus turned to Hermes for help. The younger god disguised himself as a goatherd and approached Argus, playing such sweet music on his flute that the monster dozed off. Seizing the chance, Hermes snatched up a boulder and killed him with a blow to the head. As a memorial to him, Hera later placed Argus's eyes in the peacock's tail.

Hera had been watching Hermes. Furious, she sent a gadfly to torment the cow, which ran off in a wild flight to escape the insect. Finally it reached the sea later known as the Ionian. Leaping in, the beast swam all the way to Egypt.

There Io's fortunes improved. She was turned back into human shape by Zeus, and in due course bore him a son, Epaphus.

---

of Paris (see page 65), it was Hermes who led Paris to the divine beauty contest, after he had been elected as arbiter.

Zeus in particular made use of Hermes's services, seeking his aid in compromising situations. When the nymph Callisto bore him a child, he entrusted the baby to Hermes for safekeeping from Hera's wrath. He asked Hermes to rescue Io from Argus, the monstrous guardian that Hera had set over her (see above).

Hermes also helped the other gods. When Ares was overwhelmed by two giants, Otus and Ephialtes, who managed to imprison him in a great bronze jar, it was Hermes who sneaked in to secure his release. After Dionysus's mother, Semele, was consumed by flames because she

demanded to see Zeus in his glory, Hermes saved the life of the infant god by rescuing him from the fire (see page 91). He also put the newborn Heracles to Hera's breast, whose milk could confer immortality on the human. In this instance, though, his efforts went unrewarded. The baby bit the breast, earning the goddess's hatred and causing her milk to spurt across the heavens, where it created the galaxy known as the Milky Way.

In such myths, Hermes's role was ancillary. Yet in ancient Greek ritual and religion, there are indications that Hermes had a more significant role to play. Initially he was a pastoral god. Literary references also suggest that originally he might have been a Master of Animals, with dominion over wild beasts. His cult was centered around the place of his birth—Arcadia, a mountainous region in the northern Peloponnese, where archaeological evidence suggests that he was honored as early as the second millennium BCE.

His worship may have predated that of Apollo, another pastoral deity, whose cult came to Greece with invaders from the north, probably in the last centuries of the second millennium. The story of the theft of Apollo's cattle and the gods' reconciliation may reflect a rivalry between the two cults, and their eventual accommodation. A third pastoral divinity was also associated with them: Pan, half-man and half-goat, whom some myths made out to be Hermes's own son.

Both Pan and Hermes are portrayed in myths as highly sexed. Some myths claim that Hermes was the lover of Aphrodite. One of the results of their liaison was Hermaphroditus, a youth so beautiful that the nymph Salmacis was overwhelmed by desire for him when she saw him bathing naked. The two made love so passionately that their bodies fused. Thereafter Herma-phroditus was represented with a woman's body and a man's—the original hermaphrodite.

Hermes was also associated with fertility cults. The cairns from which he originally took his name were simply standing pillars surrounded by piles of loose stones, used as waymarkers. But over the centuries, the pillar's own phallic qualities were elaborated upon, and it evolved into a column topped by a bearded head and with a horizontal projection representing the male member. These "herms" were set in public places throughout Greece, where they were thought to bring good luck. A distant memory of them may explain the Romans' fondness for using small statues of Mercury as outdoor ornaments.

Hermes's opportunism combined with his reputation for cunning to earn him a reputation as a divine trickster. He was credited with the invention of dice, and gamblers invoked his name when betting. He was also the patron of thieves. An unexpected piece of good luck was referred to as "a gift from Hermes," just as a sudden silence would be explained with the remark that "Hermes

must have entered the room." Perhaps because "herms" were often set up in marketplaces, Hermes became a god of trade, and the Romans identified him with their deity of commerce, Mercury. For luck, merchants would sprinkle water from a spring sacred to him on their wares.

This popular god's other role was as Hermes Psychopompus, literally "the conductor of souls" who led spirits to the Underworld after death. The responsibility perhaps reflected his original incarnation as a god of roads, because in early times graves were commonly dug by the wayside; in addition, as the god of boundaries, he was naturally able to cross what was for humans the biggest boundary of them all. This role also combined well with his duties as a divine messenger to whom, alone of the Olympians, Zeus had accorded free access to all three worlds—Olympus, Earth, and the Underworld.

The Greek master sculptor Praxiteles crafted this marble statue of Hermes holding the infant Dionysus c. 400 BCE. Hermes saved the baby from Semele's body after she had been burned to ashes by the sight of Zeus in his glory.

Gods of Hearth and Home

While much of Greek religious observance was public, Roman religion radiated outward from the home. To the average householder, the most important gods were not the Olympians but intimate guardian spirits who resided in the home and needed propitiation if domestic peace and prosperity were to be assured.

This 1st-century CE statue shows a *lar*, a Roman household god, holding a drinking horn aloft. *Lares* were often depicted in this way, pouring wine from drinking horns, and such statuettes were found in almost every Roman home.

The religious urge behind the Romans' domestic ritual was uncomplicated. In an uncertain world, householders sought to win good luck for their families and to ward off evil by paying respect to spirits who they thought watched over their fortunes, and who could be malevolent if neglected.

Foremost among these unseen watchers were the *lares*, represented by small statuettes kept in a cupboard shrine that occupied an honored place in every Roman living room. Generally conceived of as the spirits of dead ancestors, they looked after the households they lived in. Family members would pray to them daily and would make small offerings to them, typically of incense or wine.

Similar reverence was paid to a second group of domestic guardians, the *penates*, who took their name from the *penus,* or store cupboard, and watched over the provision of food. They were also represented by small statues, made from clay, ivory, silver, or gold depending on a family's means. A small part of every meal was set aside for them, and they were also often provided with a salt cellar. In return they were expected to keep the larder full.

The shrine of the *penates* was located beside the hearth, the focal point of the Roman home. Besides providing light and warmth, the hearth served as a sacrificial altar to the goddess Vesta, the greatest of all the household divinities. The fire within it was always kept alight in her honor; if it was extinguished, it had to be ritually rekindled with a spark struck from a fire-wheel rather than relit from an existing flame. The head of the family offered prayers before the hearth each day and made offerings of fruits, oil, and wine.

Vesta, the Roman goddess of the hearth, was closely identified with Hestia, Zeus's elder sister, who had the same responsibility. Hestia herself was among the most revered of the Greek gods, and the only one never to have become involved in wars or disputes of any kind. As a result, there were few stories about her. In her youth she was wooed by Poseidon and Apollo, but she turned both down, swearing to remain a virgin. Thereafter all the other gods treated her with respect. Originally counted among the twelve Olympians, Hestia was displaced in later centuries by Dionysus. The mythographers explained this by claiming that the self-effacing goddess voluntarily resigned her position to the younger god in order to escape from her family's eternal quarrelling.

In Rome, however, Vesta, unlike Hestia, never faded from public view. In the city, a beautiful circular temple was dedicated to her, where her sacred fire burned eternally. The temple was tended by the Vestal Virgins, young girls honored to be chosen from the city's noblest families. As the name indicated, each one took a vow of chastity: if one of them broke the oath, she would be buried alive in an underground cell, where she was left to starve or suffocate.

Two-Faced Janus

A god of doorways and beginnings, Janus was usually depicted with two faces looking in opposite directions— forward and backward, inside and out.

The two faces of Janus decorate a Roman coin, *c.* 235 BCE.

Janus was a Roman original. While almost all other Italian gods came to be identified with a Greek counterpart, there was no appropriate equivalent for Janus because his attributes were unique.

Janus's origins were ancient, possibly predating the arrival of the Latin-speaking peoples in Italy. Some mythographers claimed that he and Saturn had jointly reigned from a city on the Tiber River, creating a golden age of peace (see page 36).

By historic times he had become firmly entrenched in people's homes as the god of the threshold. It is unclear whether he took his name from the word *janua*, meaning door or gate, or if the word derived from him. Householders looked to him to keep out evil spirits, and prayed to him daily.

Janus, as the patron of beginnings, was also associated with the New Year, and the first month of the year was named after him. Presents and visits were exchanged in his honor on the first day of the first month. Later he took on a wider role in the state. A legend told how he once helped the Romans by making hot springs gush out to scald an enemy who was attacking the Capitol. A shrine was later dedicated to him in the Forum, whose four entrances were always left open in time of war.

The Path Through Life

Greeks and Romans alike recognized that other powers besides the Olympians had a bearing on people's lives. From the Fates and the Furies to the goddess Fortuna, these lesser deities could play a decisive part in determining individual destinies. In fact, some were considered even more powerful than the Olympian gods.

Tyche, the Greek personification of Chance, stands pensively, holding the emblems of her power. In one hand, she grasps a cornucopia overflowing with rewards for the fortunate. With the other, she steers the rudder of destiny. The statue dates from the 2nd century CE.

The Olympians were mighty gods, but none was omnipotent. In the *Iliad*, for example, Zeus at one point laments the fate of a favorite warrior doomed to die in battle—hardly the words of an almighty being. Greek thinkers came to believe that there must be an even mightier force, whose dictates the gods themselves had to obey. They called this force *Ananke*, Necessity, or "what has to be," and an awareness of her iron laws lay behind much of Greek literature. In Aeschylus's *Prometheus Bound*, the hero states that Zeus himself could not alter what was set down by the agents of Necessity.

The goddess Necessity was a cold, stony-hearted divinity, but she had a more attractive rival—Dike, or Justice. Dike was probably the creation of the poet Hesiod; he claimed that she was Zeus's daughter by Themis, one of the Titanesses. At the time, the word *dike* was used to describe that which was customary more than that which was just. Gradually, however, it took on its present meaning of fair arbitration. Although Dike was dear to poets and earned the admiration of Plato, she remained largely an abstract concept, never attaining the recognition of a popular cult.

In contrast to these philosophically conceived deities, the notion of Chance as an agent of destiny appealed to a wide section of the population. Tyche, as she was known in Greece, was luck in the shape of a woman. As such, she was usually shown carrying in one hand a cornucopia overflowing with good things for those whom she chose to favor. However, she was a capricious deity, as two further attributes emphasized. In her other hand she clutched the rudder of Destiny, which was always able to change direction, while beneath her feet a wheel turned unendingly to indicate the inconstancy of fate.

Tyche's Roman equivalent was Fortuna. Her cult-center at Praeneste (now Palestrina, twenty miles [32 km] outside Rome), one of the most important in Italy, housed a famous oracle. Her popularity was confirmed by the fact that three temples were dedicated to her in Rome itself. She also played a prominent role in the festival of Venus, the goddess of love, on April 1 each year: poor women would offer Fortuna incense in the hope that she would boost their attractions, while only upper-class women offered sacrifices to Venus.

For the most part, Greeks and Romans alike paid less attention to the goddesses who shaped the course of things than to the agents who carried out their decrees. And of these none struck a deeper chord in the popular imagination than the trio the Greeks called the Moirae, or Allotters, and the Romans the Parcae, but who are now most often known as the Fates. In origin the Fates were probably birth spirits, keeping watch over mothers and determining the destiny of newborn infants. By Hesiod's time they had acquired individual personalities. Clotho (literally Spinner) was responsible for spinning a person's thread of life when he or she was born, Lachesis (Lot-giver) determined its length, and Atropos (Inflexible), often considered the most terrible of the three, cut it off at the allotted point.

The classical mythographers were divided over the Fates' parentage. Hesiod made them daughters of Zeus and Themis, like Dike, but others, perhaps wishing to emphasize their independence from Olympian control, traced their lineage back to an earlier generation of divinities, considering them the offspring of Nyx and Erebus (Night and Gloom; see page 23), who between them gave rise to many evils.

This Roman votive leaf bearing an image of Fortuna served as an offering to the goddess in the 2nd century.

There was also disagreement about the nature of their powers. Some writers insisted that they answered to Zeus and carried out his decrees. Several myths indicated that they could even be persuaded to show flexibility—one tradition told how Apollo got them drunk to win a temporary reprieve from death for a mortal, Admetus, to whom he owed a debt of gratitude. Other mythographers insisted that their decisions were irrevocable and that neither god nor mortal could change what Necessity decreed and the Fates carried out.

Similar inflexibility was the hallmark of another supposed daughter of Nyx—Nemesis, goddess of just retribution. Initially she was a local goddess worshipped at Rhamnus, north of Athens, and in some versions of the story of Leda and the swan (see page 45), it was Nemesis, not Leda, who was raped by Zeus in disguise as a bird. Nemesis became famous for the remorseless fashion in which she pursued those who had transgressed against divine law.

She shared this quality with three other goddesses, the Erinyes, or Furies, who also tracked down wrongdoers with implacable persistence, regardless of the motives that had driven the individuals to commit their crimes (see page 52). According to Hesiod, the Erinyes were born of the Earth, Gaia, from drops of blood that fell on her when her husband Uranus was castrated by their son, Cronus (see page 27). Perhaps because of this ill-starred origin, they devoted themselves to punishing those who had committed crimes against their own kin, specifically those who had murdered blood relatives. Artists portrayed them as old, ugly women. Like all Fate's agents, they were objects of fear, reflecting the pessimism that underlay much of Greek and Roman thinking about destiny.

107

The Realm of the Shades

The Greeks and Romans were in agreement that after death souls went to the Underworld, somewhere far beneath the Earth. There, where the sun never shone, the dreaded god Hades ruled a kingdom that few were anxious to visit.

The earliest written accounts of the Underworld are found in the Homeric epics, and the picture they paint of life after death is not a pleasant one. Homer's dead are restless shades without strength or will, bearing the marks of the disease or injury that killed them. For example, in the *Odyssey*, the once great Achilles bemoans his fate as one of the ghosts, claiming that he would rather be a poor man's slave on Earth than a ruler of the dead.

There were, however, other prospects for the souls of the deceased. A few favorites of the gods were carried off to the Elysian Fields, lying somewhere at the ends of the Earth, where they spent their days in a sunny paradise. In contrast, wicked individuals who directly offended Zeus were

imprisoned for eternity in Tartarus in the depths of the Earth to suffer the torments of the damned.

For the next thousand years or more, the Greeks and Romans continued to accept this broad threefold division of the Underworld. But the rules that operated in Hades's domain gradually changed. As the Greeks' moral consciousness altered, reward and punishment after death became less a matter of divine whim and more a question of what individuals had deserved during their lives.

Much of the change came about as a result of the activities of the Greek mystery religions. The cult of Eleusis (see page 58) taught that its initiates could earn a place in Elysium. The Orphics added

In this Etruscan funerary relief from the 5th century BCE, the deceased is carried to the Underworld on horseback as servants of Hades look on.

Orpheus

Nowhere in world myth are the themes of love, death, and creativity interwoven as poignantly as in the story of Orpheus and Eurydice.

The son of a king of Thrace and the muse Calliope, Orpheus was a great poet and musician. The music he made was so sweet that wild beasts and even rocks and trees would follow him when he was playing.

Orpheus's young bride was the beautiful Eurydice. However, they had not been long married when she stepped on a snake, whose venom killed her.

Distraught at the loss of the woman he loved, Orpheus determined to have her brought back to life. Carrying only his lyre, he went to the Underworld to plead with its ruler, Hades, for Eurydice's release. He sang of love as a force that even Hades could not resist, and explained that he was determined not to leave the shades of the dead without his wife.

When even the damned wept at his song, Hades agreed that Eurydice could return with Orpheus on one condition: that he should not look at her until both had left the Underworld. Orpheus guided his wife by striking notes on his lyre as they toiled up the dark path. But at the last moment, his longing to see Eurydice overcame him. He turned to embrace her, only to see her slip back into the shadows with a piteous cry.

Overwhelmed by this second bereavement, Orpheus returned to Thrace, where he hardened his heart against women. This, and his attachment to Apollo, aroused the anger of the wild Maenads, female followers of the rival god Dionysus. In one of their crazed orgies, they fell upon the poet and tore him limb from limb, throwing his head into the river Hebrus.

Orpheus and Eurydice gaze sadly at each other, as Hermes waits to guide her dead soul to the Underworld, in this 5th-century BCE carving.

Even then, Orpheus was not to be silenced. The head floated, still singing, down to the sea, where it was carried by currents to the island of Lesbos. There it was finally laid to rest in a cave, where it served as an oracle for all who came to consult it.

a belief in reincarnation. In their view, each soul was born ten times, and each life-cycle totaled one thousand years, most of them spent in the Underworld. Before returning to Earth for the next cycle, each soul had to drink the waters of Lethe, the river of forgetfulness, leaving all know-ledge of the afterlife behind.

While the cultists added new dimensions to ideas of the afterlife, the poets were refining people's views of its layout and features. By the third century BCE the realm of Hades had been well mapped, and most citizens had a clear idea of what to expect after death.

The first essential step was burial, since the unburied were condemned to roam the upper world as ghosts. Once the formality of interment was completed, the soul set off on the first leg of its journey, guided by the god Hermes in his role as the Psychopomp, or conductor of the dead (see page 103).

Hermes led souls to the underground river, sometimes identified as the Acheron, more often as the Styx, that marked the boundary of Hades's realm. The only way to cross the stream was by ferry. The ferryman Charon, a disheveled figure, arbitrarily selected those spirits he would carry across and those who had to wait. The fare was an *obol*, a small coin; relatives were careful to ensure that one was placed in a dead person's mouth before burial, because those who arrived penniless were condemned to wander along the riverbank.

The gates of Hades's realm across the stream were guarded by a fierce watchdog, three-headed

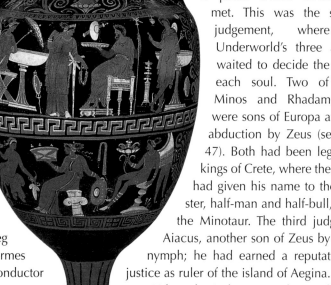

This 5th-century BCE Greek vase is decorated with a scene of feasting in Elysium. Among the guests is Eros, bottom right with wings.

Cerberus. Before the palace of Hades lay two springs. One contained the waters of Lethe, or Forgetfulness, and the other the Waters of Remembrance, which gave access to the ranks of the blessed. One of the rewards of following a mystery religion was that initiates were advised which spring to drink from.

Eventually the spirit reached a place where three roads met. This was the seat of judgement, where the Underworld's three arbiters waited to decide the fate of each soul. Two of them, Minos and Rhadamanthus, were sons of Europa after her abduction by Zeus (see page 47). Both had been legendary kings of Crete, where the former had given his name to the monster, half-man and half-bull, called the Minotaur. The third judge was Aiacus, another son of Zeus by a river nymph; he had earned a reputation for justice as ruler of the island of Aegina.

When the judges passed a verdict, the soul was dispatched down one of the three roads, which led respectively to Elysium (now located in Hades's domain), the Asphodel Fields—the Greek equivalent of Purgatory—and Tartarus. Ideas about the first two destinations had changed little since Homer's day. The real terror that assailed the dying was the thought of being condemned to take the road to Tartarus, increasingly thought of as the destination of sinners.

Tartarus was a pit so deep that it was said that an anvil dropped from Earth would take nine or ten days to reach the bottom. Much of it was in total darkness. Within its bounds, wrongdoers faced eternity under the worst torments. One was Ixion, who had killed his future father-in-law, then tried to carry off Zeus's own wife; his fate was to be stretched forever on a wheel of fire. Others suffered the misery of striving endlessly to perform tasks that could never be completed. Sisyphus, who had seized his brother's throne and betrayed Zeus's secrets, had to keep pushing a huge boulder up a steep hill, only to see it roll down each time he neared the top.

Tantalus stood accused of a peculiarly horrible crime. As a test of the gods' omniscience, he had served up the flesh of his own son at a banquet to see whether they could tell it from ordinary meat. His penalty was to stand, tormented by thirst, in a pool of water that receded when he stooped to drink; meanwhile fruit that would have satisfied his hunger hung from a bough that remained eternally just out of reach.

Tartarus's horrors endured in a long lineage of colorful accounts. They were described by the Roman poet Virgil in the first century BCE. Thirteen hundred years later, Virgil's poetic vision was in Dante's mind when he wrote his *Inferno*, although by then Tartarus had been subsumed into Christian notions of Hell. Few concepts were so little altered by the triumph of Christianity as that of the eternal punishment of the damned.

The Cave of Somnus

The god of Sleep was a minor divinity who particularly appealed to the classical poets. They pictured him sharing a gloomy cavern near the River Styx with his brother, Death.

Known to the Greeks as Hypnos and Thanatos, the two sibling deities are more familiar today in their Roman incarnations, Somnus and Mors. Ovid described their home as lying beyond the reach of the sun's rays in a remote and quiet valley. Its mouth was clogged by poppies whose drowsy scent suffused the heavy air inside its shadowy depths. There Somnus, a handsome youth with a crown of poppies around his brow, dreamed away the days on an ebony couch hemmed in by black drapes. His principal assistant, Morpheus, hovered by his side, and above his head flitted dreams, waiting to be carried by Mercury, the gods' messenger, to sleeping humans.

Meanwhile, in a remote corner of the cave, sat a very different figure. Somnus's companion was Mors, or Death, dressed in a black cloak over impenetrable armor and with the face of a corpse. His eyes were always fixed on an hourglass to note when the sands of life were running out for someone—when they stopped he would venture forth to cut down another mortal victim.

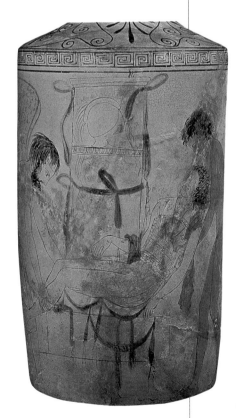

A Greek vase dating from the 5th century BCE shows Hypnos (Sleep) and Thanatos (Death) carrying a dead man to the Underworld.

THE VOLCANIC MUSEUM

When Italy's Mount Vesuvius erupted in 79 CE, burying Pompeii and Herculaneum under a lethal hail of ash and cinders, it cast over the devastated cities a preserving blanket that largely halted the usual processes of decay. The result was that when excavation began almost seventeen centuries later, buildings and even wall paintings were found to have survived in a surprisingly intact state, with even their colours unfaded. Most of the artifacts uncovered are secular and decorative, but a few reveal tantalizing glimpses of the rites of ancient mystery religions.

Above: Stepping stones set at intervals along a Pompeii street permitted pedestrians to cross the road without being soiled by the mud and refuse that clogged it in ancient times. Wagons had to steer around the obstacles.

Above: Seen from the Tower of Mercury, the ruins of Pompeii stretch towards Naples almost like a deserted and overgrown suburb of the modern city.

Right: The peace of a Pompeii garden belies the horror of the destruction nearly two millennia ago. In ancient times, such gardens would have been ornamented by statues of gods and nature spirits.

Left: The remains of a temple to Apollo are reminders of Pompeii's piety. A replica of his statue today stands amid the ruins. Along with Venus and Hercules, the legendary founder of Pompeii, Apollo was considered one of the city's guardians.

Above: This monument to the emperor Vespasian stood outside a temple constructed in his honor. Like other Roman emperors, Vespasian was deified during his lifetime. The relief carving shows a scene from a sacrifice conducted when the temple was consecrated.

Above: Pompeii's amphitheater was large enough to seat the entire population of the city. It was home to gladiatorial contests, which had their roots in early Etruscan funerary rites.

Right: Arches and columns suggest the affluence of the city in the years before the disaster. Arches often acted as entrances to prominently sited religious sanctuaries. They were thought to be guarded by Janus, the Roman god of thresholds.

Below: A 1st-century CE fresco from Pompeii shows a simple altar being made ready for a sacrifice. The large bowl would have been used to collect the blood of a slaughtered animal. Public and private altars were found throughout Herculaneum and Pompeii.

The houses of well-to-do Romans were generally built around a central courtyard, or atrium. This example, *(above)* is from the House of the Mosaics in Herculaneum. A fish pond was located in the center of the living space. A mosaic on one of the atrium walls shows Neptune with his wife, the sea nymph Amphitrite *(left)*. Mythological subjects were common themes of domestic decoration. Each residence would also have contained a shrine to its household deities.

Right: The finest of all Pompeii's wall paintings are contained in a 62-foot-long (19-m) frieze in the Villa of the Mysteries. These depict scenes sacred to the cult of Dionysus. This detail shows the education of the young god.

Below: A fresco from the House of the Vettii in Pompeii shows Cupid's attendants gathering flower petals. Images of Venus and her companion Cupid were common in the city, because the goddess was one of its guardians.

STORIES OF LOVE AND TRANSFORMATION

Tales of metamorphosis—of magical changes of form—are common in both the Greek and the Roman legacy, and they provide some of the most moving and most memorable of the classical myths. The first surviving metamorphosis stories are found in the Homeric epics, but the tradition is certainly much older. Many of these myths were once used to explain natural phenomena by suggesting connections between divine or human events and the observable but often mysterious phenomena of the natural world. For example, the constellations hinted at the forms of heroes or creatures transformed into patterns of bright stars by the gods. The shapes and colors of various species of birds, flowers, and trees were related to stories about humans who had, for one reason or another, been transformed. Thus the native Mediterranean hyacinth, with its almost blood-colored purple leaves, inspired a story about a young man named Hyacinthus who was loved and accidentally killed by Apollo; the god, in his grief, turned the youth's bleeding body into a flower, immortalizing his memory.

Below: The Roman Cupid was depicted as the playful infant familiar today. Here he is carved into a decorative border on a 3rd-century CE sarcophagus.

Long after early scientists and naturalists began to explain the natural world in purely physical terms, transformation myths continued to be prized for their entertainment value. Stories of love and passion had always been enjoyed by the Greeks and Romans, whose gods were prodigious lovers. Zeus himself often changed his shape in order to seduce women who caught his roving eye, just as Hera often transfigured those women to foil Zeus in his amorous pursuits. In the last three centuries BCE, tales of metamorphosis became so popular that writers began to add new shape-changing themes to existing stories. Later, in the first century CE, the Roman writer Ovid wove together many of these tales in his poetic work, the *Metamorphoses*. For him, and for his readers, the myths became celebrations of the joys and terrors of sexuality and the tenderness of human affections, told for the sake of pure diversion.

Opposite: Having vowed to maintain her chastity, Daphne desperately resisted Apollo's attentions. To guarantee her safety, her mother Gaia transformed her into a laurel tree. Here the moment of her transformation is visualized by Antonio Pollaiuolo in 1475.

117

Cupid and Psyche: An Allegory of Love

Apuleius, the second-century CE Roman author of *The Golden Ass*, included in his book a love story about a god and a beautiful mortal, using traditional characters in a new way and combining elements of myth and folktale. His story of Cupid and Psyche is at the same time an entrancing fairy tale and an allegory about the nature of love.

A master storyteller, Apuleius presents his tale of love with refreshing humor. He uses many traditional elements of myth, with a cast of characters including the famous divinities Venus and Cupid and a plot revolving around a love affair between a god and a mortal. In addition, the pronouncement of an oracle plays a key role in moving the plot along. However, the story also contains many elements that are more typical of popular folk tales, including a mysterious bridegroom, evil sisters and a cruel mother-in-law. It begins with the words, "Once upon a time" and ends happily, as romantic love overcomes all obstacles.

At the same time, Apuleius uses the characters of Cupid and Psyche to develop a long-standing philosophical enquiry about the nature of love. Both characters can be seen as essentially symbolic. The heroine's name, Psyche, means "soul" in Greek, and according to one popular interpretation the story examines the relationship between the soul and love (because Cupid, or Eros, is the divine incarnation of the power of love).

Concepts of love and the soul underwent many changes over the centuries. In the Homeric epics, the soul was seen as a person's life-force. Visually, it resembled the person but was intangible, and it inhabited the body; at death it departed the earthly frame and took its place in the Underworld still possessing the outward appearance of the dead person, like a kind of ghostly after-image. From the fifth century BCE, artists, poets, and philosophers, including Plato, began to see a profound connection between love and the soul, Eros and Psyche. Around the third century BCE, they started to depict Eros as inflicting torments on Psyche, reflecting the familiar idea that true love has to prove itself by surviving pain. Apuleius picks up this theme of the miseries of love.

In Apuleius's story, Psyche was a young princess so beautiful that awestruck admirers began to worship her almost as if she were a goddess, undertaking pilgrimages to her home and making offerings and sacrifices to her. Venus, the Roman goddess of love and beauty, resented the attention paid to this mortal woman, and she commanded her son Cupid to cause the princess to fall in love with someone wholly unsuitable—a wretch, beggar, or criminal.

Meanwhile Psyche's father had consulted the oracle of Apollo (see page 83) because he feared that the gods would be angered by the devotion his child was attracting. He was also concerned about her marriage prospects, since men, intimidated by her beauty, found her unapproachable; her two less remarkable sisters were already suitably wedded. The oracle offered little comfort. It

Eros tempts a woman with a plate of fruit. The Greeks depicted him as an alluring young man, as in this 4th-century BCE vase painting.

commanded the king to prepare Psyche for a wedding and then leave her alone on the top of a mountain where she would become the bride of an evil spirit.

Accompanied by a mournful wedding procession, Psyche set out for the appointed crag. Nightfall found her alone, in the dark, weeping and waiting to meet her monstrous husband. But no monster appeared; instead she was carried off by the west wind to a magnificent palace in a lush, green woodland.

In exquisite surroundings, invisible hands dressed her to receive her suitor and served her a bridal banquet, accompanied by the sweet music of unseen players. Eventually she retired, alone, to her bedroom. There, in pitch darkness, a lover came to her, but he was so gentle that her fear evaporated, and she regretted his sudden departure just before the break of day. This pattern repeated itself the next day and the next, and Psyche was happy even though her new husband vanished each morning.

For a long time Psyche was content in her palace with the unseen servants for company. One night, however, her husband warned her that her sisters were searching for her but that she must ignore them. They would only try to persuade her to discover his identity, but if she looked upon his face she would instantly lose him. Nonetheless, Psyche missed her sisters and begged him to allow her to see them. Despite his deep misgivings, her husband was unable to resist her pleading. Warning her again to tell her sisters nothing about him and to resist becoming curious about his identity, he conceded to her request.

Although the visitors were at first delighted to discover that Psyche was not dead, they soon

A Roman mosaic from the 3rd century CE shows Cupid peacefully dozing, while Psyche holds his magical bow for safekeeping. In her discovery that Cupid was her mysterious husband, she ran the risk of losing him forever.

became jealous of her good fortune and conspired against her. They told her that she was mad to love someone she had not seen, and that the child she was by now carrying had a right to know the truth about its father. They teased and worried her so much that she lost confidence in her husband, finally making up her mind to discover for herself who he might be.

That night Psyche concealed a lamp under her bed and when she knew her husband was asleep, she drew it out. The flame illuminated the divinely beautiful body of Cupid, the winged deity of love himself. The god had been so overcome by her loveliness that he had disobeyed his own

119

mother and constructed the elaborate plot in order to marry her. In her joy and excitement, Psyche let a drop of hot oil fall on Cupid's shoulder. The pain of the burn woke him and he took flight, injured, betrayed, and furious.

When Psyche reported all this to her sisters, they were delighted. Each secretly visited the crag where Psyche's adventures had begun, to beseech Cupid to accept her in Psyche's place. Then they jumped off the cliff, expecting to be wafted by the west wind to the palace of love. But their greed and treachery were promptly punished and they crashed to their deaths on the rocks below. Psyche herself, inconsolable at the loss of her husband,

tried to commit suicide by throwing herself into a river, but the river washed her ashore. She then set out to search for her husband.

The distraught girl at first attempted to find comfort and advice from the shrines of Demeter and Hera, but neither goddess was prepared to risk the wrath of Venus. Hearing reports of her son's love affair, Venus was furious that he had dis-obeyed her orders. Her anger was further inflamed when she learned that Psyche, a mortal, was expecting Cupid's child—her grandchild.

Venus sought Psyche out and punished her with a series of seemingly impossible tasks. The girl had to sort a whole roomful of mixed grains,

The Golden Ass

The Metamorphoses, _more commonly known as_ The Golden Ass, _is the only narrative in the form of a novel in Latin that has survived in its entirety. It is an entertaining and magical adventure story that influenced many later writers._

The Golden Ass describes the adventures of Lucius, a young man whose curiosity about magic leads him into trouble when he is accidentally turned into a donkey. Wandering in search of a way to be transformed back into his human form, Lucius is haunted by bad luck, but his many misfortunes serve only to improve his character and disposition. Finally he is turned back into a human being by the goddess Isis (see page 15). The tale is amusingly told in the style of a popular romance and remains a good read today.

Apuleius, the author of the text, was a highly educated man, who studied extensively in Carthage, Athens, and Rome and

was known as a poet, rhetorician, priest, and philosopher. He wrote a number of successful books, including some serious philosophical treatises and other more comical works, of which The Golden Ass is the most famous. It won broad acclaim in its own day, and was popular for centuries, even though many of its messages conflicted with Christian doctrine. In fact, the lasting popularity of Apuleius's story led St. Augustine, the influential fourth-century Christian theologian, to warn against praising the author too highly.

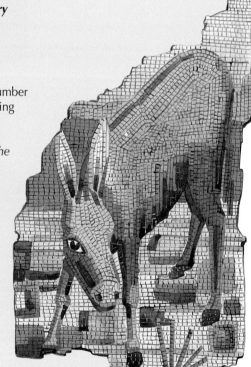

and to bring Venus some wool from a flock of man-eating sheep and a jar of water from the River Styx. But the powers of nature were so moved by Psyche's love for Cupid that they helped her fulfil the goddess's commands. First an army of ants separated the grain. Then a reed advised her that she could collect wool from the briars against which the sheep had brushed. Finally an eagle, sacred to Zeus, fetched the water from the Styx.

Venus was not appeased and set Psyche one more task, which this time seemed sure to be fatal. She ordered the young woman to go down to the Underworld and bring up a jar of Persephone's cosmetic ointment. Since no mortal could return from the realm of Hades alive, Psyche reconciled herself to death and climbed a high tower, planning to throw herself from it. But again she was offered supernatural help. The tower, moved by her unhappiness, gave her instructions on how to reach Hades safely and on how to escape.

Images of Eros or Cupid often adorned jewelry. Here a bust of Eros is used on a gold medallion decorated with garnets, delicately crafted in Greece in the 3rd century BCE.

Psyche brought the precious ointment to the surface of the earth, but then foolishly thought that if she used some of it herself she might win back her husband's affection. When she opened the jar, the scent of the ointment overcame her and she fell into a death-like trance.

Now, however, Psyche's devotion and grief and her obedience to Venus moved Cupid to forgiveness, and he rushed to her side to revive her. While Psyche took the jar to Venus, Cupid sought the permission of Zeus to remarry his faithful partner, this time with the full ceremony of a heavenly wedding. Zeus agreed and granted Psyche immortality, inviting her to live on Olympus. Psyche and Cupid dwelled there in eternal joy with their daughter, Voluptas (Pleasure).

The Uses of Transformation

In Ovid's stories, love and metamorphosis usually go hand-in-hand. Some, like the tale of Pygmalion, present the process of change as a recompense for religious virtue, while in others it is used to reward faithful lovers. The gods can also impose transformation as a punishment for faithless or wicked mortals.

In the tale of Pygmalion, Ovid celebrates the power of love and also adds a moral message: the gods will act on behalf of mortals who treat them with respect.

Pygmalion was a skilled sculptor who lived on the island of Cyprus, a place sacred to Venus, the Roman goddess of love. As a young man he had spent some time on Cyprus in the city of Amathus where the women were vulgar and debauched. This disgusted the artist, who became so convinced that women were sinful by nature that he took a vow of chastity.

He remained alone and directed his energy into his work, crafting his statues with great devotion and becoming very successful. Eventually he decided to carve a statue that would represent everything good and beautiful about the female form. In this he succeeded far too well: the ivory woman he created was so beautiful that he fell passionately in love with her.

The artist embraced and kissed the statue, moving it from his studio into his house and eventually into his bed at night. He dressed it in women's clothes, adorning it with jewelry, and treated it with all possible care and devotion. But gradually he realized that this was not enough: he so loved the image of the woman he had created that he wanted her to become human so that she could love him in return. Night after night he knelt in front of his statue, beseeching Venus to grant him this extraordinary favor and transform the statue into a woman of flesh and blood. At last, the goddess was moved by his desperation and his respect for her powers; moreover she was delighted that someone who had once despised physical love and the beauty of women, both areas of her special patronage, was now under their spell. She decided to grant his request.

One night as he caressed the statue, he felt a tremor run through it. His beloved grew warm and soft beneath his fingers, changing from a statue into a living, breathing, beautiful woman. His prayers were fully answered when he looked into her eyes and saw his own love returned by a companion who would remain faithful to her maker all her life. With the blessing of Venus, the lovers were married, and together they had a son Paphos, who grew up to found a famous city, in Cyprus, named after himself.

Many of the myths that Ovid told, however, did not have the sort of religious or ethical content found in the tale of Pygmalion. Often the gods rewarded faithful lovers whose ardor was

The Venus de Milo presents an ideal of feminine beauty in a lifelike form. Carved *c.* 100 BCE, it has captured the world's imagination over the centuries.

Ovid

Publius Ovidius Naso was born at Sulmo, about 93 miles (150 km) from Rome, in 43 BCE. His father intended him to be a lawyer and had him educated with that in mind, but even as a young man, Ovid wanted only to be a poet.

Ovid came of age just at the time of the great literary flowering that took place during the period of peace and stability that marked the beginning of the reign of the emperor Augustus. He became a friend of such poets as Virgil, Horace, and Propertius, and was probably part of the imperial circle itself.

He wrote a number of books of poetry, including the scandalous *Ars Amatoria* (The Art of Love), a collection of erotic verse in the form of a manual on how to win and keep a lover.

However, his most impressive work was the *Metamorphoses*, a mythological history of the world from creation to the reign of Augustus, containing more than two hundred and fifty separate myths. All the tales are woven with great ingenuity into a continuous and coherent whole. Although he drew largely from the works of Greek dramatists and poets, Ovid was more poet than scholar and he often added episodes of his own, or even whole new stories.

Before completing the final version of the *Metamorphoses*, Ovid was banished from Rome, in part because of the shocking nature of the *Ars Amatoria*. He was not happy with his revisions to the *Metamorphoses* and burned the manuscript in disgust. The text only survives today because his friends held additional copies. Although he continued to pour out poems and letters after his banishment, the essential spark had gone out of his life and he died, sad and lonely, in 17 CE.

The great charm of the *Metamorphoses* not only made it popular in its own time but enabled it to survive into the Christian era. It was probably the most widely read non-Christian text throughout the Middle Ages, and scarcely a single major European poet before this century failed to owe its author a debt. It is thus thanks to Ovid that so many of the classical stories have survived in living, imaginative form. History has justified the final, boastful lines of the *Metamorphoses*: "I shall live to all eternity, immortalized by fame."

untinged by any particular virtue. Several of Ovid's stories are about tragic lovers who are comforted or reunited by a magical transformation, often at the moment of death.

One such is the story of Alcyone (or Halcyon, as she was also known). She was the daughter of Aeolus, the guardian of the winds. When she grew up she married Ceyx, king of Trachis. They proved an exemplary couple, famous both for their hospitality to strangers and for their mutual affection.

Ceyx set sail from Trachis to visit the oracle at Delphi, but was shipwrecked and drowned on the journey. Alcyone was advised of this disaster in a dream, and the next morning, disturbed and fearful, she went to the beach and searched the shoreline for signs of wreckage. There the tide washed her dead husband up to her feet. Grief-stricken, she attempted to drown herself in order to rejoin him, but the gods could not bear the death of so loving and faithful a couple. The two were instantly transformed into seabirds. In

Alcyone's honor, the gods also provided, each winter, a week of calm seas, the Halcyon Days, so that the couple could brood their young in a nest that floated safely on a smooth, windless sea.

The two characters, Alcyone and Ceyx, feature in another, very different myth, part of an older tradition. In this version, they were deeply in love and happily married. However, this time their contentment made them overconfident and they began to call each other Zeus and Hera. This presumptuousness angered the Olympian first couple, who turned the two mortals into seabirds as punishment. It was a typical Ovidian touch to rework the story in such a way as to reward their faithful love for each other.

Romantic passion was not the only form of love that was rewarded by transformations. The Pleiades, the cluster of stars sometimes called the

Medusa was born a human and became a beautiful young woman. However, she was transformed into a monstrous Gorgon, with snakes for hair, by Athena, after she thoughtlessly defiled the goddess's sanctuary. Here, she is depicted in a Hellenistic relief at a temple in Didime, in modern-day Turkey.

Seven Sisters, were the daughters of Atlas, supporter of the heavens, and Pleione. The sisters were famous for their beauty and notorious for their affairs. Only one of them, Merope, married a mortal—Sisyphus, king of Corinth. The other six all took lovers from among the gods. Three of them—Electra, Taygete, and Maia—were Zeus's mistresses, and bore him sons. Poseidon and Ares also admired the sisters and had several children by them. But despite the favor of the gods, all seven of the sisters died of grief over the death of their brother, Hyas, and their sisters, the Hyades.

Zeus was so touched by this sisterly devotion that he turned them into stars. It was said that the reason why one of the stars in the cluster is so much less bright than the other six is that Merope's light is dimmed by the shame of having had only a mortal husband instead of a divine lover.

Metamorphosis was used by the gods not only as a reward for virtue but also as a punishment, often for neglecting their worship or transgressing their commands. Mortals who directly challenged one of the Olympians, or claimed to be equal or superior to them, were frequently punished for their affrontery by being changed into various animals or plants. For example, Athena turned Arachne into a spider for daring to compete with her at weaving (see page 73).

Medusa, the Gorgon, was born human, not a monster, but a mortal, unlike her horrible sisters Stheno and Euryale. While she was still young and beautiful she had an affair with Poseidon, but the couple rashly made love inside a shrine to Athena. The goddess was outraged partly because Poseidon was often her rival, but more because she was herself a virgin, so it was particularly improper that one of her sacred places should be used for such impious practices. As a consequence of this single thoughtless act, Medusa was harshly punished. Her lovely hair was turned into live snakes and her beautiful face was made so hideous that anyone who looked upon it was immediately turned into stone.

In some stories, such as the poignant but terrible tale of Procne and Philomela, transformation is at the same time punishment and reward. These two women were the daughters of Pandion, king of Athens, and were devoted to each other. Procne married Tereus, king of Thrace, and had a son, Itys, by him. She badly missed her sister and urged her husband to go to Athens and bring Philomela to Thrace for a visit. Tereus obliged, but as soon as he saw Philomela, he became crazed with desire for her. Once he had her safely in Thrace, he raped her and then cut out her tongue so that she could not report his treachery. After imprisoning her in a for-est, he went home and pretended to his wife that on arriving in Athens, he had learned that Philomela had died.

In the meantime, unable to speak or escape, Philomela wove the story of her agony into a tapestry and sent it to her sister. When Procne discovered the truth, she figured out a way to find the missing girl. She joined the cult of Bacchus (see page 92) so that she could roam the country among his followers until she had located and freed Philomela.

Together they then plotted a horrible revenge against Tereus. Even though she had always been a loving mother, Procne decided to sacrifice her own son for her sister's honor. She murdered and dismembered the boy and then the two women cooked him in a stew, which they served to Tereus. When Tereus finished eating the meal and commented approvingly on the tenderness of the meat, Procne revealed to him that he had eaten his own child. Driven mad by the discovery, he drew his sword to kill the two sisters, but they were instantly transformed into birds with red splashes among their feathers like stains from Itys's blood.

The Greeks, on whose story Ovid based his retelling, believed that Procne was transformed into a nightingale, mourning her son with sad cries, while Philomela was turned into a screeching swallow. The Latin authors reversed this pattern of transformation, making Philomela the nightingale, a more reclusive, forest-dwelling bird, and Procne the angry-sounding swallow. How-ever, in both traditions Tereus himself was metamorphosed into a hoopoe, whose crest gives a royal appearance and whose huge curved beak was thought to resemble the sword he had drawn against his wife, still thrust forward as if expressing his desire for revenge.

Above: **A hoopoe, whose sharp curved beak was thought to resemble the sword that Tereus had used to try to kill his wife and her sister.**

Aphrodite and Adonis: A Myth of Love and Death

It was not just mortals whose lives and passions were affected by the complications of love and by the metamorphoses that are such a particular mark of Greek and Roman mythology. Divine transformations were far from frivolous—in fact, they could have far-reaching consequences on the gods as well.

The complicated myth of the love affair between Aphrodite and Adonis shows how the Olympians, too, were vulnerable to the pain of love. This moving story contains many of the thematic and narrative elements typical of classical mythology. It presents a moral lesson and shows the way in which metamorphosis was used in the tales to explain natural phenomena.

The daughter of Cinyras, king of Assyria, was a beautiful young woman called Myrrha; according to some accounts she was also the granddaughter of Pygmalion and his statue-bride (see page 122). Myrrha was so proud of her appearance that she refused to pay respect to Aphrodite, the goddess of beauty. Angry that she was not duly honored, Aphrodite caused Myrrha to fall in love with her own father. This was a desperate fate, since the taboo on incest was extremely powerful throughout the Greek world.

Myrrha was unable to contain her lust, and since she knew her father would reject her advances, she sought the assistance of her nurse to deceive him. Together the two women made him so drunk that he had no idea what he was doing. After twelve nights of illicit pleasure, Myrrha became pregnant by him.

When Cinyras discovered what had happened he was so shocked and angry that he could

The Greeks admired male beauty, of which Adonis was an ideal. Handsome figures were often depicted sensuously, as in this bronze sculpture of an unknown man, *c.* 430 BCE.

Aphrodite is depicted in a pensive mood in this bronze head, dating from the 2nd or 1st century BCE, found at Satala (now Sadagh) in eastern Turkey.

think of no solution other than to kill his daughter. Perhaps because Myrrha had not sinned of her own volition, the gods intervened and protected her from her father's righteous anger. She was turned into a myrrh tree, and her tears of repentance became its precious, sweet-smelling gum.

In time the tree split open and deep within the trunk a baby, Adonis, was revealed. He was of such extreme beauty that Aphrodite herself was beguiled by him. Worried that so ill-conceived but exquisite an infant would be in danger in the world, the goddess hid him in a chest, which she sent to Persephone, queen of the Underworld, for safekeeping, asking her never to open it. Persephone, surprised to be asked a favor by a goddess with whom she was often in competition, betrayed Aphrodite's trust. Overcome by curiosity, she lifted the lid and saw the child. She, too, was taken by the boy's beauty, so much so that she refused to return the chest to Aphrodite.

A quarrel followed, and finally the two goddesses turned to Zeus for arbitration. He decreed that Adonis should spend four months of the year with each of the goddesses and could decide for himself how to spend the final third—in fact, as an adult, he chose to pass this extra time with Aphrodite. Another version has it that Zeus was too shrewd to risk the anger of either goddess and gave the responsibility of judgement to Calliope, one of the Muses. This made Aphrodite bitterly angry, and in revenge she caused the death of Calliope's son, Orpheus (see page 109).

127

Adonis grew up to become a handsome, lively, and intelligent youth. He was Aphrodite's faithful lover and they spent all the time they could together. His only other interest was hunting, about which he was almost fanatical. Aphrodite constantly begged him to limit his sport to the pursuit of small game, but despite his promises he was unable to resist a challenge, and one fateful day he was killed by a wild boar. Either Hephaestus, Aphrodite's husband, or Ares, her lover, had disguised himself as the boar in order to take revenge against the usurper of her affections.

Aphrodite was inconsolable, because she had loved the young man truly and passionately. To immortalize his memory, she transformed his spilled blood into red anemones that honor his death with their perennial blood-colored flowers.

A resurrection cult of Adonis started in Cyprus and spread throughout Greece and later Rome. The cult's followers worshipped him as a god of fertility, seeing the harvest as the time when he left the Earth to spend his appointed period with Persephone in the Underworld. In Athens, the cult's devotees mourned the youth's death not only with ceremonial dirges sung over the youth's effigy but also by planting "gardens of Adonis," in which the seeds of sprouting plants were sown in shallow soil so that they sprang up with great speed and then died just as promptly.

Adonis, although famous in the classical world as the epitome of male beauty, was infrequently depicted in art. This Etruscan monument showing the moment of his death is a rare example. A hunting dog sits faithfully by his side.

The Sad Tale of Echo and Narcissus

The story of Echo and Narcissus is one of the best known of all the classical myths of transformation. A typical Ovidian metamorphosis tale, it combines a portrait of a man suffering from a very human trait, excessive self-love, with explanations of two natural phenomena, the mountain echo and the early-flowering narcissus.

Echo was a nymph from Mount Helicon, a range of mountains in Boeotia in central Greece. This area was also favored by the Muses, who raised and trained the young nymphs who lived there. Thus Echo was well prepared for the service of Hera, and became a member of the goddess's retinue. Despite her duty to Hera, however, the maiden was always sympathetic to Zeus in his amorous pursuits, even though she was never his mistress. Instead, she assisted him in his philandering by distracting his wife's attention.

Whenever Zeus wished to engage in a flirtation or seduction, he would inform Echo and she would then involve Hera in light-hearted conversation, diverting her so that she failed to keep her usual sharp eye on her husband. This ruse proved highly successful, since Hera loved gossip. Echo would chatter away charmingly, and Zeus was free to indulge himself in the company of attractive nymphs or maidens.

At last, however, Hera saw through the trick and was very angry. To punish Echo, the goddess afflicted her with an inability to start a conversation or introduce any new topic of discussion. For eternity Echo was limited to repeating the very same words that someone had addressed to her. Embarrassed, she fled to the most desolate woodlands and valleys of Mount Helicon, but she continued to delight in talking. She would stalk everyone who happened to find their way into her wilderness, and would then repeat, mournfully, anything that they might say.

In the meantime a young man called Narcissus was courting a doom of his own, in his case through excessive pride. Narcissus was the son of the nymph Lirope and the river god Cephissus. While he was still a baby his mother had sought foreknowledge of her son's future by visiting the infallible seer Tiresias.

There are several explanations for Tiresias's prophetic abilities. According to one legend, as a young man, Tiresias had killed two mating snakes and had been magically metamorphosed into a woman. Eight years later, he did the same thing and was restored to his original male form. Because he had experience of being, in turn, both man and woman, Hera and Zeus asked him to settle an argument. When Tiresias sided with Zeus, Hera was so angered that she blinded him. But because his answer had vindicated Zeus, the god gave Tiresias the gift of prophesy in compensation. Another myth tells how Tiresias was blinded after seeing Athena bathing, and that she then gave him the gift of prophecy.

The nymph Echo is shown dancing with a satyr—a fellow nature spirit—on this 5th-century BCE Greek vase.

Narcissus lived a solitary existence in the forests of Mount Helicon. A Greek artist shows him equipped with a bow and arrow in this mosaic from the 2nd century CE. Cupid, symbolizing love, stands by his side.

Tiresias became the most famous seer in Greece, although when Lirope consulted him, he had only recently received the gift of prophecy and had not yet established his reputation. In reply to Lirope's query as to whether Narcissus would live a long life, Tiresias answered: "Yes, if he never knows himself." At the time, this seemed a senseless response, but years later, when Narcissus met his fate, people would remember the seer's words and appreciate his powers to foretell the future.

Narcissus grew up to be both ravishingly handsome and outrageously arrogant. Many people, both men and women, fell in love with him, but he despised them all and rejected their advances with cruel disdain. Taking delight in his own company, he ranged the woodlands of Mount Helicon totally indifferent to the pain and grief of his suitors. Finally, driven to distraction, one of his

spurned lovers asked the gods that Narcissus should suffer the same pain that they did: unrequited love.

This prayer came to the attention of Nemesis, the goddess of vengeance and retribution. She followed Narcissus, and as he passed a still pool of water, she afflicted him with a fierce thirst. When he bent over the water to drink, he saw for the first time his own reflection in the quiet water, as though in a mirror. Now, as Tiresias had prophesied, Narcissus knew himself—although he did not understand that it was his own reflection. He believed instead that he was at last looking at a man worthy of his love. From that moment he remained hopelessly in love with his own image. When he bent toward it, it seemed to respond and to move eagerly toward him, but just as he was about to kiss the adorable face, the image would disintegrate and he would have to wait until the water was calm for his beloved to return.

The nymph Echo saw Narcissus by the pool and promptly fell in love with him as he murmured words of passion and devotion to his own reflection. Hampered by her curious affliction, she tried to seduce him by repeating his own last words, believing them to be directed at her since she could see he was alone. At first he was amused and charmed to hear his endearments repeated by another voice, but gradually, absorbed in his contemplation of himself, he began to ignore her. She, however, was so besotted by him that her unrequited love eventually wore her out. Her body faded away and only her voice was left, haunting wild, rocky places, eternally echoing every sound she heard.

The only thing Narcissus cared about was the unresponsive but devastatingly beautiful man whom he could see, so near but unobtainable, in the water in front of him. He lay, rooted to the spot beside the pool, languishing for love of the image within it, until he too faded. Finally the gods took pity on him, and he was transformed into the narcissus, blooming early in the spring, whose flowers always hang downward, always reaching towards their reflection in the water.

Apollo and Daphne

For the nymph Daphne, daughter of Gaia, as for Narcissus, transformation was neither reward nor punishment.

Once Cupid had a quarrel with Apollo. The child god was offended because Apollo told him he was too young for archery and should leave bows and arrows to men. In revenge he shot Apollo with one of the arrows that caused its victim to fall in love with whomever the winged god chose. To perfect his vengeance, he selected Daphne.

Daphne was a virgin nymph, in mourning for the prince Leucippus. He had fallen in love with her, and when she rejected him he disguised himself as a woman so that he could hunt with her. As companions in the chase, they became close, loving friends. Unfortunately, one day after he, Daphne and some other nymphs had been hunting together, the women decided to bathe. The nymphs stripped naked, but Leucippus invented an excuse not to. Teasingly, the assembled nymphs tore off his clothes and his true sex was revealed. The virgin nymphs immediately assumed that Leucippus's intentions were dishonorable. Before Daphne could intervene, they killed him.

After this Daphne not only swore to remain a virgin, but also began to shun all human company, hunting alone. So Apollo had little hope of persuading her to return his intense passion.

Nevetheless, burning with love and desire, the god was determined to have his way with her. Apollo used all his considerable charm to seduce Daphne, but she rejected him. Then, impatient and frustrated, he attempted to rape her. She fled terrified into the forest, but

Apollo, now enraged as well as lustful, followed her. The chase went on until Daphne realized that she could not escape.

Despairing, she cried out to her mother for help. Gaia acted swiftly to protect her beloved daughter: just as Apollo reached out to seize her, Daphne was transformed into a laurel tree.

Apollo's lust was replaced by shame, and he humbly broke off a single branch of the tree to wear in his hair. From that day on, the laurel was sacred to Apollo, and he awarded a crown made from its branches as a prize to be awarded to the finest musicians and poets, in honor of Daphne's beauty

Daphne is depicted with a figure believed to be her father, in a Greek mosaic found in Paphos, Cyprus.

Baucis and Philemon: Virtue Rewarded

Ovid's tales of simple goodness and innocent love can be deeply affecting, as in the story of Baucis and Philemon, who are rewarded by the gods for their generosity of spirit and deep love and affection for each other.

One day, bored on Olympus, Zeus and Hermes decided to disguise themselves as humans to see what life was like for mortals. In town or city, they found it virtually impossible to obtain a bed for the night or even a meal, despite the fact that offering a welcome to strangers was central to the Greek code of conduct.

In Phrygia, a region of Asia Minor, they spent a day in a village where they could obtain neither food nor lodging, even for money. Tired and hungry, they arrived at a peasant hut on a hill just outside the village, the home of an elderly married couple named Baucis and Philemon.

To the gods' relief, they were at once given shelter, and Baucis offered them a meal, apologizing for its frugal nature, but assuring the visitors that it was the best she had and that she and her husband would share it with them. They sat down at the table and Philemon offered a prayer of thanksgiving to Zeus for their life, their contentment and the honor of their guests. While Baucis served what food there was with grace and generosity, Philemon opened their only wine vessel

The Code of Hospitality

Hospitality to strangers as well as invited guests was regarded as a sacred duty in ancient Greece—and one that the gods could be expected to reward.

Next to religious and family obligations, and valiant conduct in war, the codes of hospitality toward guests were given the highest value. The duty of the host was to act as though the guest were kin: what one would provide for a relative, one should also provide for a stranger. There were formal procedures of welcome, with rules about washing, clothing, and feeding, and limits on the curiosity about the identity or destination of a chance arrival.

Since every safe journey had to be celebrated with a sacrifice, the host was expected to provide the guest with the equipment. Any necessities furnished to a guest were treated as gifts.

Guests were supposed to act as though they were members of the family. This meant, in particular, becoming actively involved in any feuds between the host family and its enemies and not seducing any women of the household. Breaches of this etiquette frequently caused

trouble. For example, the Greeks' anger at Paris's seduction of Helen, which led to the Trojan War, was all the greater because Paris had been her husband's guest at the time.

After receiving hospitality, the guest was linked to the host in a bond of "guest-friendship," which was theoretically as binding as a blood relationship would be. The two owed each other eternal fidelity, and each was liable to support the other in time of war or other trouble.

and poured the thin, sour liquid into a serving bowl. Then they ate, drank, and chatted.

Not surprisingly after their previous experiences, Zeus and Hermes were touched and delighted by the welcome. At first they said nothing, but as the evening went on Baucis and Philemon noticed that the bowl of wine remained full no matter how deeply the guests drank. Suddenly it dawned on them that these were no ordinary travelers and, humbled and alarmed, they fell to their knees, apologizing for not having recognized their divine visitors.

The two gods then admitted their true identities. They reassured the frightened couple before leading them out of the house and farther up the hill. When Baucis and Philemon turned to look back they found that their valley was now filled with water, and that the inhospitable village had completely disappeared beneath a glimmering blue lake. Their little cottage had become a small temple on its shore.

Zeus praised them for their piety and generosity and offered them any reward they might

choose. Although they could have asked for riches or power, they requested only that they be allowed to tend the shrine as its priests. Zeus, impressed by their modesty, urged them to ask for something more, and after consulting with each other they decided on a special favor: that they should die at the same moment since neither one of them could endure the thought of having to live on without the other.

Zeus had no difficulty in agreeing to this request. He promised them that their wish would come to pass, then he and Hermes disappeared, leaving the couple shaken but delighted. Philemon and Baucis lived together by the lakeside for many years as priest and priestess of the temple. They remained as humble and as pious as they had ever been, and never failed to offer hospitality to anyone who passed by. Because the shrine was well-attended, their days of poverty were over.

Eventually, tired but contented, they were changed at death into two trees, in acknowledgement of their virtue. Philemon became an oak, and close beside him Baucis lived on as a linden.

THE LEGACY OF THE OLYMPIANS

The classical gods have been a long time dying. The first voices questioning their authority were raised within a few centuries of their initial description by Homer and Hesiod, yet the names of the greatest of them are still familiar to most people today.

The earliest assault on the divinity of the gods came from the Greek natural philosophers. From as early as the sixth century BCE, thinkers sought explanations of the universe that sidelined the Olympians even when they did not directly deny their existence. Thales, history's first recorded metaphysician, is said to have declared that water was the basic substance of creation and that gods permeated everything. Anaximenes traced everything back to air and called it "god." Heraclitus of Ephesus, on the other hand, considered fire to be the primordial element, and ridiculed purification rites using the blood of sacrificed animals as tantamount to washing in mud.

Hard on the heels of the philosophers came the moralists. Of these, Xenophanes of Colophon was the Olympians' harshest critic. "Homer and Hesiod," he wrote accusingly, "have ascribed to the gods all things that are a shame and a disgrace among men: thefts and adulteries and deceptions of one another." It was a view that was to be echoed many times in later years as the power of the gods waned.

As the Greek world grew wider and more sophisticated, the doubts expressed at first by a handful of intellectuals spread to some other sections of the population. The process accelerated in Roman times, when the Olympian deities came to be manipulated as creatures of the state. Rulers were shameless in using the gods for their own ends—a process that culminated, logically enough, in the deification of the emperors themselves and the establishment of cults in their honor.

A religion that could be so easily tailored for political ends was unlikely to command deep

The Forum in Rome, built in stages from the 7th century BCE, was the center of public life in the ancient city and housed many temples. Today, it is one of the modern city's most visited tourist attractions, a testament to the sway the ancient world still holds over our imagination.

personal commitment. Most citizens continued to pay their respects to the Roman deities as patriotic duty, much in the same way that today people rise to their feet when their national anthem is played. But those seeking a more spiritual dimension to their lives increasingly looked elsewhere for enlightenment. Some found what they were seeking in philosophy, and others in a profusion of unfamiliar Eastern sects, such as that of Isis (see page 15), that promised personal salvation.

Out of the tumult of rival faiths, one eventually emerged triumphant. Although it took three centuries for its message to spread across the Empire, the final victory of Christianity was surprisingly quick. In 313 CE the emperor Constantine personally adopted the Christian faith and removed all civil restrictions on its persecuted followers. Although he continued to tolerate the worship of the old gods, Christianity rapidly became the official religion of the state.

Yet paganism, as the older religion came to be called, was by no means dead. In the mid-fourth century the Olympians were reinstated under the emperor called Julian the Apostate by his Christian enemies. Julian restored all the old rites, including animal sacrifice, and for a brief period the tide of Christianity was rolled back. But the emperor was killed within two years of coming to power, and the pagan reaction collapsed.

Scholars in European monasteries helped to preserve the classical texts for posterity. In this 15th-century Book of Hours, the Four Evangelists are shown as if they were mediaeval scribes.

Christianity finally gained supremacy in the Roman Empire at the end of the century under the emperor Theodosius the Great. In 391 CE, he prohibited sacrifices and the visiting of temples, and the next year the worship of the ancient gods was banned. Oracles were closed and temples were destroyed or converted to the uses of the newer faith.

The church itself proved more pragmatic in its attitude to the major pagan festivals. The most popular of all was the Saturnalia, dedicated to the god Saturn (see page 36). A time of merrymaking, feasting, and the giving of presents, the Saturnalia was celebrated in the week after December 17. The fourth-century decision to celebrate Christ's birthday on December 25 (there was no record of the actual date) was itself based on the supposed birthday of the Persian god of light, Mithras, whose cult was strong in Rome, and the new festival of Christmas was to take on many of the features of Saturn's feast.

More importantly for the long term, Christianity inherited both a culture and a language from the ancient world. Its priests were required to be literate, and that meant being able to read and write Greek and Latin. So the early Christians continued to study the classical texts, even though they still regarded them as full of error. The widespread and respected study of astrology also remained inextricably linked with

The Lincoln Memorial in Washington, DC, completed in 1922, was modeled on the Parthenon, the 5th-century BCE Athenian temple dedicated to the goddess Athena. Inside the building is a 20-foot-high (6-m) statue of Abraham Lincoln; an equally imposing statue of Athena dominated the interior of her temple.

the names of the classical gods. Even after the last vestiges of the western Roman Empire were swept away by the barbarian invasions in the sixth and seventh centuries, the Church, and in particular the monasteries, helped to preserve Latin manuscripts, thus safeguarding the memory of the old deities.

There were other channels for the survival of the myths outside western Europe. The eastern half of the Roman Empire, with its capital in Constantinople (present-day Istanbul), was never overwhelmed as the western had been, and the great Byzantine civilization flourished there for a further thousand years. Although it too was Christian, it always regarded itself as the inheritor of the classical world, and its libraries preserved many works. In addition, the Byzantine Empire kept alive the knowledge of Greek, which gradually faded in the West.

The Islamic world also played a vital part. From the seventh century onward, Arab conquerors created an empire that stretched from Syria to southern Spain. The caliphs encouraged the translation of classical works into Arabic, pro-

viding another medium for their passage into the modern world.

In the West, however, the Church gradually stopped seeking exemplars in the classics, looking instead to the Bible as the sole source of moral wisdom. The destructive Viking raids of the ninth and tenth centuries accelerated this process by breaking up many monastic libraries.

It was not until the eleventh and twelfth centuries that the flame of scholarship again burned bright. But when it did, the classics were available for rediscovery. Latin literature was the first, because knowledge of ancient Greek had been almost entirely lost by that time.

By the fourteenth century, Italian intellectuals such as Petrarch, the sonnetteer, and Boccaccio, the author of the *Decameron,* were once more studying Greek so as to be able to read Aristotle, Plato and Homer in the original. In 1371 Boccaccio produced *De Genealogia Deorum* ("On the Genealogy of the Gods"), the first of many new compendia of classical mythology. After almost a thousand years in which a knowledge of the old divinities had been regarded as dangerous at best, he dared to praise the moral value of the Greek and Latin poets.

The classical heritage came back into its own during the Renaissance in the fifteenth century. Greek came to be studied as well as Latin, because the fall of the Byzantine Empire to the Turks in 1453 brought a flood of Greek-speaking scholars hurrying westward as refugees. The children of the wealthy followed courses in grammar, poetry, rhetoric, history, and moral philosophy, all of them drawn from classical texts. Poets scattered their lyrics with references to classical mythology, and artists chose subjects for their paintings from the myths. The ability to recognize a classical allusion became the mark of a cultured individual.

For the next four centuries, a knowledge of the classical world and its gods was the common intellectual currency that linked the educated classes of the Western world. It was only with the twentieth century that interest in the classics once more began to decline. A new emphasis on practical and vocational studies drove Latin and Greek from their dominant position in the higher-education curriculum. Had their survival depended on the educational system alone, the gods would have faded away.

Yet the psychological and symbolic power of the classical stories survives in literature and the arts. Twentieth-century writers have continued to draw inspiration from the myths, and in so doing have emphasized their continuing relevance for the modern world. The Irish dramatist George Bernard Shaw found the plot for one of his best-known plays in the story of the sculptor Pygmalion, who fell in love with a statue he had

The modern Olympic Games are a reminder of the classical tradition of athletic excellence. At each opening ceremony, the flame is lit by a torch kindled in Olympia, Greece.

created; the work reached even wider audiences as the musical *My Fair Lady*. French playwrights Jean Giraudoux and Jean Anouilh both had successes with dramas drawn from Greek sources. France's Jean Cocteau and North America's Tennessee Williams made use of the Orpheus myth: Cocteau in his film *Orphée*, and Williams in the play *Orpheus Descending*.

At a more popular level of traditional culture, Venus and Cupid still reign unchallenged as personifications of beauty, love, and passion. No Valentine's Day would be complete without cards illustrated with hearts transfixed by Cupid's wilful arrows of desire.

The long-term cultural effects of the retreat from classical studies have yet to be seen. But it seems clear that the Olympians and their myths will not die away, because they are too deeply embedded in Western culture. In the coming centuries they will no doubt go on providing what they have already done for so long: an alternative world of the imagination peopled by characters of universal appeal.

137

Glossary

ambrosia The food of the Greek gods.

amphitheater An open-air arena, where spectator sports were often held in ancient Rome and Greece.

caduceus The staff carried by Hermes, entwined by two snakes and with wings on top.

carnage Great slaughter or injury, usually during a time of war.

centaur A creature that is half man, half horse.

cornucopia A horn of plenty; a symbol of abundance or nourishment represented by a horn shaped container that is overflowing with food.

deity A supernatural being; usually a god.

demi-god A mythological figure whose one parent was a god, while the other was human.

emigrant One who moves from one country or location to another, usually for economic reasons.

frieze A long stretch of painted or sculpted decoration, usually placed above eye level and included as part of the architecture of a building.

idyllic Happy, peaceful, or picturesque.

mortal One who is not born of the gods.

mythographer One who compiles ancient myths.

nectar The drink of the gods.

nymph A nature deity, represented by a beautiful maiden who dwells (and controls) the forces of nature.

oracle A person who gives a wise opinion, usually about things to come.

pantheon The collective gods of a group of people or culture.

prophecy A prediction of something to come.

satirist One who writes works that hold up human vices to ridicule or scorn.

trident A three-pronged spear, usually belonging to Poseidon.

For More Information

Acropolis Museum
15 Dionysiou Areopagitou Street
Athens, Greece 11742
Web site: http://www.theacropolismuseum.gr
E-mail: press@theacropolismuseum.gr
Museum focused on the archaeological findings of the Acropolis of Athens.

British Museum
Great Russell Street
London, England
WC1B 3DG
Web site: http://www.britishmuseum.org
World-famous art museum, featuring collections of artifacts from ancient Greece and Rome.

Metropolitan Museum of Art
1000 5th Avenue
New York, NY 10028

(212) 535-7710
Web site: http://www.metmuseum.org
One of the largest and finest art museums in the world, including an extensive collection of ancient Roman and Greek artifacts.

Museo della Civilta Romana
piazza G, Agnelli, 10
00144 Rome, Italy
Web site: http://en.museociviltaromana.it
Museum showcasing artifacts from the Roman Empire.

National Hellenic Museum
801 W. Adams Street, Suite 400
Chicago, IL 60607
(312) 655-1234
Web site: http://www.333southhalsted.org
E-mail: info@hellenicmuseum.org
The only major museum in the U.S. dedicated to telling the story of Greek history, culture, and art from ancient times to today.

University of Pennsylvania Museum of Archaeology and Anthropology
3260 South Street
Philadelphia, PA 19104
(215) 898-4000
Web site: http://www.penn.museum
Museum with three gallery floors featuring materials from Egypt, Mesopotamia, Canaan and Israel, Mesoamerica, Asia, and the ancient Mediterranean world.

Web Sites

Due to the changing nature of Internet links, Rosen Publishing has developed an online list of Web sites related to the subject of this book. This site is updated regularly. Please use this link to access the list:

http://www.rosenlinks.com/grom

For Further Reading

Burkert, W. *Greek Religion*. Oxford: Blackwell, 1985.

Cook, A.B. *Zeus*. Cambridge: Cambridge University Press, 1940.

De Coulanges, Fustel. *The Ancient City: A Study on the Religion, Laws and Institution of Greece and Rome*. Charleston, California: Forgotten Books, 2010.

Dodds, E.R. *The Greeks and the Irrational*. Berkeley: University of California Press, 1951.

Dowden, Ken. *Religion and the Romans*. London: Duckworth Publishers, 2008.

Easterling, P.E., and John V. Muir (eds). *Greek Religion and Society*. Cambridge: Cambridge University Press, 1985.

Festingiere, A.J. *Personal Religion Among the Greeks*. Berkeley: University of California Press, 1960.

Finley, M.I. *The World of Odysseus*. Harmondsworth: Penguin, 1991.

Fox, Robin Lane. *The Classical World: An Epic History from Homer to Hadrian*. New York: Basic Books, 2008.

Grant, Michael. *The Myths of the Greeks and Romans*. Harmondsworth: Penguin, 1995.

Guerber, H. A. *The Story of the Greeks*. North Carolina: Yesterday's Classics, 2006.

Guthrie, W.K.C. *The Greeks and Their Gods*. London: Methuen, 1950.

Guthrie, W.K.C. *Orpheus and the Greek Religion*. Princeton: Princeton University Press, 1993.

Hard, Robin. *The Routledge Handbook of Greek Mythology*. London: Routledge, 2003.

Hoffman, M. and James Lasdun (eds.) *After Ovid*. London: Faber, 1994.

Kirk, G.S. *The Nature of Greek Myths*. Harmondsworth: Penguin, 1990.

Kitto, H.D.F. *Greek Tragedy: A Literary Study*. London: Methuen, 1961.

Mikalson, J.D. *Athenian Popular Religion*. Chapel Hill: University of North Carolina Press, 1983.

Morford, Mark. *Classical Mythology*. Oxford: Oxford University Press, 2010.

Nilsson, N.P. *A History of Greek Religion*. Oxford: Clarendon Press, 1949.

Ogilvie, R.M. *The Romans and Their Gods*. London: Chatto, 1969.

Perowne, S. *Roman Mythology*. Twickenham: Newnes, 1983.

Powell, Anthony. *Ancient Greece*. New York: Chelsea House Publishers, 2007.

Rose, H.J. *Ancient Roman Religion*. London: Hutchinson, 1948.

Scullard, H.H. *Festivals and Ceremonies of the Roman Republic*. London: Thames and Hudson, 1981.

Tripp, E. *Handbook of Classic Mythology*. New York: Harper & Row, 1970.

Index

Page numbers in *italic* relate to illustration captions. Where there is a textual reference to the topic on the same page as the caption, italics have not been used.